FORT LANGLEY

Birthplace of British Columbia

FORT LANGLEY

Birthplace of British Columbia

B.A. McKelvie

Afterword by Charles Lillard

Porcépic Books Limited
Victoria, B.C.

This edition is published by Porcépic Books Limited, 4252 Commerce Circle, Victoria, B.C., V8Z 4M2, with the assistance of the Canada Council and the B.C. Ministry of Municipal Affairs, Recreation and Culture.

All photographs and maps, unless otherwise mentioned, are courtesy of the British Columbia Archives and Records Service.

Decorations by C.P. Connorton.
Cover design by Arifin Graham.
Production editor: Cheryl Smiley.

Canadian Cataloquing in Publication Data

McKelvie, B.A. (Bruce Alastair), 1889-1960.
    Fort Langley, birthplace of British Columbia

      ISBN 0-88878-298-5
      1. Fort Langley (B.C.)—History.   I. Lillard,
Charles, 1944-   II. Title.
FC3849.F6M24 1991   971.1'33   C91-091168-1
F1089.5.F6M24 1991

In Memoriam
Bruce Alastair McKelvie

This is something like the apostolic succession;
this is the laying on of hands.
—Oliver Wendell Holmes

For
Benjamin Daniel Lillard

Contents

1
Coming of the Sky People

The lower valley of the Fraser River opens like a great, green fan from the point where the river bursts from the gorges of the Coast Mountains and moves majestically through 95 miles of lush lowlands to empty itself into the Strait of Georgia. In the last 40 miles of its gentle way it tastes the brine of sea tides. This estuary, since the beginning of time, was the larder of its littoral. Even today it is an important sustaining factor for those who live along its shores.

It is a turbid stream. It deposits earth torn from the far Interior on the ever growing deltas at its several mouths. But the Fraser was not always muddy. In the days before the big islands were formed it was crystal clear. Sturgeon and salmon could see from its pellucid depths the approach of native fishermen with net and spear. Consequently, there was a scarcity of food at all times and the human inhabitants of the valley found it difficult to exist. Then it was that Qals, the Transformer, took pity on the people—so say the storytellers of the Halkomelem—and darkened the waters, although to do so he was forced to slay one of his brothers. Ever since the fish have been confused and are easily taken, and the natives have lived prosperously with little effort.

There were several names for the Fraser River. The Indians knew it as Stalo. When white men first came to locate upon its banks they knew it as Cowichan River, a fitting designation, because it was the rendezvous of the mighty Cowichan division of the Salish linguistic stock. Indians came in their thousands to this gathering place when the two-horned mountain T'lagunna—known today as the Golden Ears—beckoned. When this grand bold peak could be seen from the sea, dwellers on the coast knew that the salmon were crowding up to their spawning grounds. Then the Semiahmoo and the Songhee and the Saanich pushed their way up the winding, twisting little Nicomekl River, and portaged over to an equally crooked little stream, known to them as the T'salkwakyan—now called the Salmon—to share the silvery harvest of the river.

The Cowichans—now Coast Salish—were a mighty people, scattered, in scores of villages, all the way from lower Puget Sound to Seymour Narrows and Yuculta Rapids, down the coast to the Fraser, and up that river to the mountain barrier. There were many important divisions and numerous sub-divisions of this people. Each was autonomous, and they were frequently at war, one with another, but they were allied against the dreaded Kwakiutl, and more particularly the Yuculta—Euclataw—branch of that piratical nation. It was an alliance of fear. Repeated raids in their long, swift canoes by warriors from the intricate channels between Vancouver Island and the mainland north of the Strait of Georgia had taught the less warlike Cowichans to cower at the very name of their oppressors.

Halkomelem—Stalo—was the name of the collection of sub-tribes of Cowichan strain who peopled the fan of the Fraser delta. There were some 17 bands of them, of whom the Kwantlen were most powerful. Siam-Kwantlen—or Royal Kwantlen—they arrogantly called themselves. They ruled the stretch of river from the points of its division below present day New Westminster to the domain of the Katzie. They claimed that in earlier times they also held dominion over Lulu Island.

They were intruders in this domain. Once the Coquitlam, a powerful sub-tribe, held sway over a goodly part of the river from Skaiametl, a big village which stood where New Westminster is now located. The invading Kwantlen had conquered the Coquitlam and had held them in subjection. Across the Fraser River, the land near the site of the old community of Brownsville was low and marshy. Beyond it was a hill of earth and gravel. The lordly Kwantlen conceived the idea of creating a summer village on the flat, so they made the Coquitlam carry filling from the hill and forced them to construct a site for the town, which they named Kikait. It was a pleasant place, was Kikait, according to the tales of the old people.

The woods were alive with game in those days. Bands of elk stalked majestically across forest openings, fleet deer grazed in the many natural meadows, while the industrious beaver continually engineered fish-ponds and new communities of his kind on the little streams that drained forest land and swamp. The Indians rarely disturbed forest creatures; the river gave them an abundance of food-stuffs. They were a happy people in a bountiful land. Only the constant dread of the Yuculta and the internecine disputes of their own people of Cowichan stock disturbed the Kwantlen, who became fat and fearful from easy living, and lost the will to resist the invaders from the north.

Strange tales reached the Kwantlen from the sea. The Semiahmoo and Songhee brought improbable stories with them in the summer of 1792. They told of gigantic white-winged canoes, so big that in the distance they looked like snow-capped islands. These stupendous craft were carrying strange, supernatural men with light faces and wearing peculiar clothing, the like of which had never been seen before. There had been but little else discussed when the people met that autumn on the Saan-a-sant—Pitt—River where the Katzie were hosts each year during the digging of Indian potatoes, amid great festivity. Strange people from far away had been heard of from tribes on the outer sea coast. The Squamish peoples had actually met similar ghostly visitants the previous year.

Squamish chiefs boasted of having been aboard one of the mighty canoes, which approached like a floating island. In fact, they were Sky People declared the men from Howe Sound, who told how they had been given shining discs, such as some of the Sky People had on their clothing. The chiefs could not attach these to their Indian garb. The discs were hard and could not be pierced by instruments of bone or stone.

The Kwantlen doubted these tales. Surely if the Sky People were roaming about the country they would visit the mighty river.

Years passed, and stories of Sky People were forgotten. No longer did visiting tribesmen tell such improbable tales when the big fires blazed in the vast cedar buildings along the Saan-a-sant.

And then they came: the Sky People came to the Kwantlen!

It was 16 years after that summer when all were excited about the gigantic white-winged canoes. Everyone knows that four is the mystic number of the necromancers. This was four times four, a year of potent mysticism—if there was any truth at all in the stories of the ghost-men.

It was on July 2, 1808. The people from Skaiametl were luxuriating across the river at Kikait...but let the story be told as old Staquist, who was present, related it many years later:

> I was there when Simon Fraser came. All the people were frightened. They called out and ran around. Some picked up their bows and spears. Others just stood still and looked. It

was seen that some of the people in the canoes were just like those who had come in the white-winged canoes. They were not like any of the people who lived on the river, or like those who came when the salmon ran thick in the summer. The faces of some were pale; others had big beards. They wore strange clothes. They were the Sky People, we thought. They stopped out on the river for a time, then they came ashore.

We looked at them closely, and saw that the eyes of some of them were blue like the sky, and others were gray like the clouds. Yes, they must be Sky People. Their faces were light in color, but were not painted. We touched their clothes. They were strange; not like blankets made from dogs' hair, or from skins or from cedar bark.

Whattlekainum, one of the sub-chiefs, tried to talk to them, but they had strange tongues. The chief of the Sky People then made signs and we understood. He was on his way to the sea, but he would come back again. Then he went away.

When the canoe of the chief started down the river, one of the men took what looked like a crane, and put the legs over his shoulder and blew on the head of it, and made his fingers dance on the bird's bill—and strange sounds were made. Some said it was not a crane, but sticks. The noise that the man made went up the river and came back, and we thought that there were more Sky People coming.

The people of Musqueam were at war with those of Point Roberts. When they saw the strange canoes coming they thought that their enemies had crossed over by the way that the Semiahmoo came to get salmon, and they got ready to fight with them. When they saw that they were strangers, they did not kill them, but they were not friendly and the Sky People did not go any farther.

The next day they came back to Kikait and they all came ashore. Some of them took out small sticks with knobs on them and put them into their mouths. Then they took out bags and made fire, and put it on the end of the sticks and smoke came out of their mouths. We thought that they would burn up, but this did not happen, so we knew that they were supernatural.

Then the chief of the Sky People showed us what we thought was a big stick. He cut and peeled some small willows and put them up, crossed, one over the other. Then he went back some distance and pointed the big stick at the twigs. We nearly died, for fire came from the big stick and it made thunder, and the smaller sticks fell over. Everyone was frightened.

12

He talked to Whattlekainum, and made him understand that he could use the thunder-stick, and if he could knock over the small sticks, which were set up again, he could have the thunder-stick.

Whattlekainum—who was not afraid of anything—said he would try. Twice he pointed the big stick and only a flash came. Then the strange chief did something to the thunder-stick. This time when Whattlekainum pointed it, it made thunder, but it knocked him back and he fell down. He did not want to touch it any more.

Before they came to us the water had made some of the goods in the canoe wet; so the Sky chief had it all taken out and spread out to dry. Our young men became excited, for there were great treasures there—daggers, not made of bone or stone, but of metal like those of the Songhee which they had secured from the tribes on the outer sea. There were ropes there, too, not made of cedar bark or skin, and—oh, lots of things we would like to have. Some of the young men watched.

The strangers stayed all night. When it was dark they had the strange music again, and one of the men danced. Before they had come down the river, we were told later, they stopped at Squa—Chilliwack—and when the music was made there they all danced. It was so good the people all wanted to dance with them.

In the morning when the Sky People made ready for departure, some things were missing. The white chief became angry. Some of his men searched among the people and found the articles our young men had stolen. They took the things from the young men and kicked them. That was bad. It is all right to kick a squaw, but not a warrior. It makes him ashamed. So the hearts of the young men grew black inside them. When the visitors left the young men got ready to follow and kill them that night when they stopped to camp. We knew where it would be, opposite to Mount Lehman.

When Chief Whattlekainum heard this he said, 'No, do not try to hurt the Sky People; you can not kill them because they are supernatural. They come from the sky. There are as many of them as the stars. If you try to kill them, more will come and they will kill us all. You saw how they took fire into their stomachs and were not burned; you saw the thunder-stick. No, you must not do what you plan.'

Some of the old men said the words of Whattlekainum were good. But the young men who had been kicked looked black.

13

Then the chief said, 'I know that you feel ashamed because you were kicked. I feel sorry for you, so I will remove the shame. I will make you presents.' And so did Whattlekainum give away all his own belongings to the young men to keep them from killing Simon Fraser.

A mighty man was Whattlekainum. Tales of his prowess in war and wisdom in peace are told and retold amongst the remnants of the once powerful Kwantlen. He was first amongst them to welcome the return of the Sky People after another four-times-four years had passed.

Although he was a sub-chief of the Kwantlen, his mother was a sister of the chief of the Tsawwassen, near the main mouth of the Fraser river. He had been brought up by his mother's spartan people. He was roused before daybreak to plunge into the river, in all weathers. Then he had to run for miles to harden his muscles, and to practise with bow and spear.

One morning as he dashed through the woods a tremendous storm arose. Animals, frightened, ran wildly through the forest amongst toppling trees. When they saw the young Indian, they flocked about him for protection. He picked up two small wolf cubs which had become lost. Then their mother came seeking them. She bared her teeth to attack Whattlekainum when she saw her little ones in his arms, but he spoke gently to her, and pointed out that he was protecting them. She came and licked his hand. Years later, when there was a shortage of food in the village, Whattlekainum went in search of meat for his people. He found a newly-killed seal on the beach, another and then another. When his canoe was filled and he was paddling off, he noticed a big she-wolf at the river's edge, wagging her tail. The mother-wolf had repaid her debt.

Then there was the occasion when he slew the giant from Active Pass. This man, who towered above all other Indians, was a gambler, and a fearsome individual. He kept frogs in his long matted hair to fascinate his gaming victims so that they could not concentrate upon the game. All men—except Whattlekainum—were afraid of him. He knew this, and hated the young sub-chief. One night at a feast on the Saan-a-sant, Whattlekainum saw him pass his hand over the dish of food intended for the Kwantlen. Instead of eating the food the chief called one of his dogs and gave him a morsel. The dog died almost instantly. Whattlekainum fetched his bow and arrows, returned to the banquet hall and drove an arrow into the giant. Looking for the body, later, he traced the giant to a hastily-erected structure some distance from the village, to which one of his wives had removed him. This time Whattlekainum's arrow did not wound. Years after, it was said, the skeleton of the giant was found with the arrow-head firmly fixed in the spine.

Then there was the time that Whattlekainum encountered the great lizard on Lulu Island. That was the only time he retreated.

Whattlekainum lived to a ripe old age, and became the familiar of several white men who later occupied Fort Langley. He watched the erection of the first fort, saw it replaced by a second and larger one, saw that one burn, and an even more pretentious one arise from its ashes.

The second and third forts were built on a gravel ridge above the high water of the river's flood periods.

Old Tent-a-coose, the bow-legged water carrier of the fort, who had learned the lore of the river, used to tell how that gravel ridge was formed. It was away back before there were many humans, and the animals could talk. The whole area was low and flat. On one side of the marshy ground lived the Brown Beavers; on the other, the Yellow Beavers. There was a grove of cottonwood trees about the centre of the tract and the beavers were continually disputing its ownership. They decided to ask the horned mountain T'lagunna to adjudicate. The chiefs of the Brown and Yellow Beavers told the mountain their troubles.

Golden Ears listened patiently. Then he shook his head. "No," he said, "it is too difficult for me to decide; you had better ask assistance from my brother, the great White Mountain" (Mount Baker). So the beavers travelled for days and came to the great White Mountain, who heard their complaints. He pondered for a time, and then told them to remove their people from the disputed ground. When this was done he shook and rumbled, and smoke and fire came out of this crest. Then he threw out earth and gravel and it fell on the low marshy land, creating a ridge that was to be the boundary between the warring beavers. That was how the ridge was formed. It must be true. Old Tent-a-coose said it was so.

A picturesque chap was this bow-legged water carrier. His long life had been hard and adventurous. Born near Active Pass, he had been captured by the Kwakiutl in boyhood and raised in slavery. He developed great strength, for which a chief of the Clayoquot (from the west coast of Vancouver Island) purchased him. That is how it came about that Tent-a-coose saw the last moments of John Jacob Astor's vessel, the *Tonquin*.

The Indians had attacked the craft and killed Captain Jonathan Thorne and most of his crew. Several men managed to get into the cabin and held the Indians off. That night all but one of them attempted to escape in a small boat, but were subsequently captured and killed. One man remained on board. He appeared on deck and motioned for the Indians to come. They swarmed over the ship. When several hundred Indians were aboard, a tremendous explosion took place. The lone survivor had exacted a terrible revenge. About two hundred natives were killed or wounded, Tent-a-coose used to explain with a delighted chuckle—he hated the Clayoquot.

Ransomed by the Hudson's Bay Company, he was brought to Fort Langley, where he served the rest of his days. He was drowned in 1867 in the muddy waters of the river he loved.

2

Bombast, Wine and Confusion

It was a gray December day in 1813. Winter storms had lashed the coast for a week, preventing the little sloop *Dolly* from returning to Fort Astoria from HMS *Racoon* at anchor in Baker Bay at the entrance of the Columbia River.

The *Racoon* had come around Cape Horn in company with other armed vessels, intending to capture Astoria with its wealth of furs and trade goods. The ships had separated, and *Racoon* had arrived on November 30 with her guns cleared for action. Officers and men were eager for battle and their shares in prize money that would come from the conquest of John Jacob Astor's Pacific headquarters.

Braving the dangers of navigation over the Columbia River Bar—and only touching twice—*Racoon* had made Baker Bay and dropped anchor, there to be boarded, not by cowering Americans ready to thrown themselves upon the mercy of Captain William Black, but by representatives of the proud North West Company of Montreal. They shocked the captain by telling him that the establishment he had come so far to conquer now belonged to that Canadian organization, which had recently purchased the fort and all it contained.

Gradually, in the ten days that followed, Captain Black pieced together the story of happenings in the neighborhood for the past two or three years, and of the bitter rivalry that was developing for the commercial supremacy of the empire west of the Rocky Mountains.

Astor, a naturalized American citizen of German birth, had conceived the idea of constructing a monopoly in the fur trade at the mouth of the Columbia and operating from a base there by land and sea. He offered partnership in the venture to the North West Company, but the lords of the fur trade in Montreal had scorned the offer. They had pioneered the pathways across the mountains into the far west. It was plain presumption for Astor with his Pacific Fur Company to talk to them of sharing that vast wilderness beyond the continental divide. Besides, the fellow never could succeed; he was a dreamer of dreams.

But the mighty men of the fur trade, toasting to future success, boasting that their agents had challenged the might of the Hudson's Bay Company, in scattered trading posts across half a continent, did not know John Jacob Astor. While they laughed at his audacity, he worked. Soon he had induced a number of their most experienced men to join him. He prepared two expeditions for the Pacific, one to go overland and the other aboard the *Tonquin*.

The *Tonquin* was ready to clear from New York, laden with trade goods and personnel, to establish a fort before the Nor'westers realised the danger. Hurriedly David Thompson, a partner in the North West Company who had already achieved fame as an astronomer, was outfitted to dash across the continent, reach the mouth of the Columbia and there build a fort before the Astorians could arrive. It was a race, with an empire as prize.

Thompson aimed to reach the headwaters of the Columbia and follow that stream to sea. As he and his followers approached the foothills of the Rockies, the Piegan Indians threatened them. This—and unknown terrors that lurked beyond the snow-capped range—caused disaffection and finally desertion.

At last Thompson found himself with only eight followers out of his original two score or more. It was impossible now for him to complete his dash for the sea before the coming of the heavy snows. He would have to winter in the mountains. There was no turning back. So he erected a small shelter—hardly to be dignified as a "fort"—at the source of the Columbia and he and his men spent a miserable winter. With the breaking up of the ice they embarked their canoes which had been constructed during the winter.

It was April when they started. They did not know that March had witnessed the arrival of *Tonquin*. When several months later, Thompson swept down into the estuary of the Columbia, it was to find the Astori-

18

ans well on the way to completing their establishment. The Nor'westers had lost the race.

Tragedy marked the victory of the Americans. Their vessel, under command of an irascible former naval officer, Jonathan Thorne, sailed northward to traffic with the Indians. Alexander McKay—he who had accompanied Sir Alexander Mackenzie on his journey across the continent in 1793—had gone along as trader. The ship did not return. She was taken by natives of the west coast of Vancouver Island and her personnel butchered.

Captain Black was also told that in the late months of 1812 and the following year, despite many worries and anxieties, improvement had been shown and the abundant promise of the country was now being realized. Trading parties had pushed up through the Okanagan country, and established Fort Kamloops at the forks of the stream named by Simon Fraser in honor of David Thompson. The Similkameen, also explored, was a land of expectation.

The outlook had been fair indeed. And then the news had come— just how or when the captain did not learn—that United States and Great Britain were at war. The loyalty of some erstwhile employees of the North West Company was strained. Those of American birth became boastful: their country had brought George of England to ignoble defeat once; it could be done again. But the dour Scots who had lived for so long in Canada kept their peace—and doubted.

While the belated news of conflict was causing concern on the Columbia, a danger to the settlement was approaching from the sea. The influential Montreal traders who had strong political friends in London, had whispered in the ear of the government that there was a rich, fat, juicy plum to be picked from Astor's tree on the Pacific Coast. Orders were sent to the senior officer commanding at Rio de Janeiro to send naval vessels to capture the settlement on the Columbia. The *Isaac Todd*, bearing letters of marque, was to accompany the expedition. Aboard the *Isaac Todd* went John McDonald and Donald McTavish of the North West Company, to take possession of the fur fields if opportunity offered.

But something might happen. The ships might not arrive. So the crafty lads in Beaver Hall decided to minimize chances of failure, this time. J. G. McTavish and John Stuart—Simon Fraser's old companion in New Caledonia (the name Fraser gave to what would become British Columbia)—they were instructed to make all haste across the continent to the sea with a strong party. They did so, and arrived in time, reaching Fort Astoria well in advance of the British armed forces. They informed their former comrades, now in the employ of Astor, of the approach of units of the Royal Navy to blast them from their log fort, and seize the furs and trade goods.

McTavish and Stuart were sorry for their old companions—at least they said so. In order that all the effort of building the post and opening trade in the surrounding country should not be lost, the sympathetic visitors offered to buy the place and everything it contained, at—well—well, under the circumstances, of course...say about 15 per cent! The deal was made. And now, Captain Black of HMS *Racoon* and his men realized that their dreams of fat purses had vanished into the coffers of the North West Company.

Great was the wrath of the gallant captain. He had been deceived in every respect. He had visualized great glory to be achieved by battering down a strongly fortified place. When he saw the log bastions and wooden palisades, he exclaimed: "Fort! Is this what I have come so long a distance to take? I could blow it to pieces in two hours with a four-pounder!" So to him and his complaining officers and men it was a case of neither profit nor glory.

For days Captain Black munched the bitter fruit of frustration. Then he decided to act. The *Dolly*, which had been storm-bound in Baker Bay for a week, was about to return to Astoria, a dozen miles distant. Here was his opportunity. Chief Concomoly's Indians were sent in fleet canoes with messages for the chiefs of the Clatsop and Chinook and all others that might be reached, to assemble at the fort. They were to witness a great ceremony. Then in his best uniform agleam with gold braid, and with the lieutenant of marines similarly aglow, and attended by four seamen and four marines, Captain Black boarded the *Dolly*.

Arriving at the fort, the gilded officers were affably greeted by the fur traders. They were noted for their hospitality, were the officers of the North West Company. And while the captain and lieutenant dined within the officers' quarters, they announced that they had come to take possession of the place, and would be obliged if McTavish would have an inventory made of all that he had purchased on behalf of his company from Astor's men. While he had no intention of making physical seizure of the goods and chattels at the moment, it might be that a prize court in London would award him the value of the merchandise—or at least a portion of the value for distribution among his men, said Black. McTavish and Stuart were dumbfounded.

So was James McMillan, clerk, when a few minutes later Captain Black ordered that all the Nor'west engages should be armed with muskets and be drilled for half an hour. They were to form a guard of honor. So, Jean Ba'tiste and Francois and the dour Scots and half breeds who had come down the river in the Company's canoes were lined up and armed, while the men of Astor's hiring were to enact the part of the conquered. It was a ridiculous affair: so thought Tom McKay, Métis son of Alexander McKay who had perished with the *Tonquin*. Tom was already earning a reputation for courage. But men like Michel Laframboise, the interpreter, who had but lately played the role of Indian, spying upon the incoming *Racoon* from Adam's Point, were interested only in the pageantry.

Now everything was ready. The trappers and boatmen of Black's militia were marched to the platform outside the palisades, where four pieces of artillery were mounted. There, too, was the flagstaff. The armed levies were, with some difficulty, formed into the proper military formation in front of the pole. Then Captain Black ordered the British ensign lowered, and that of United States raised, only to be again lowered to the ground at his command.

As the flag of the Republic came down, and that of Great Britain was once more to be hoisted, the Captain addressed the spectators and with an all-inclusive wave of his arms declared that he took possession of the post and of the country for His Majesty King George III. Now one of the sailors stepped forward and raised the Union Jack. The spectators were ordered to cheer. The sailors, marines and a sprinkling of others did so.

Now another sailor stepped forward and presented Captain Black with a long-stemmed bottle of Madeira. Stepping to the foot of the flagstaff, the gallant captain smashed the thin glass against the pole, exclaiming in a loud voice, "I rechristen this place Fort George"—but there were no cheers, and subjects of the young republic, among the onlookers, spat. George of England was not popular with them since the days of Lexington. But there was noise, for the captain commanded the guard of honor to fire three volleys in celebration, while the marines and seamen operating the four guns blazed away three rounds from each piece to celebrate the affair. And old Chief Concomoly and the other chiefs of the Columbia looked on in wonderment at the strange antics of the white men.

Captain Black was pleased with himself. He believed that he had really accomplished something—and, at least, he had salved his wounded dignity. He had won for himself a place in history, but had irretrievably lost to the British Crown a magnificent land through his bombast and wine.

The Canadian company continued occupation of Fort George. In 1814 the inconclusive war ended by the Treaty of Ghent. The first article of that instrument stipulated that nay and all places taken by one power from the other during the conflict should be forthwith returned. The United States lost no time in demanding restoration of Astoria—for the name that had been bestowed on his "capture" by Captain Black was a constant reminder of dispossession.

Great Britain replied that Astoria had been acquired in a private deal between two private companies, and could not be regarded as a conquest. "No," replied United States's diplomats, "it was officially captured by your Captain Black, who formally re-christened it with good Madeira wine." There was no denial. It was agreed the place would be returned.

This was effected in 1818 when another ceremony was held at the flagstaff. This time J. B. Prevost, on behalf of the United States, accepted the return of Astoria and the country from Captain Hickey of HMS *Blossom* and James Keith of the North West Company. There was not so much show, nor the burning of so much powder, but all the same, men like James McMillan, and Thomas McKay were not pleased, but to Michel Laframboise it was a welcome break in the monotony so common at isolated posts.

Keith and the Nor'westers remained in possession of the place, for how long no one would predict. Prevost had hinted that the United States would soon colonize the locality. There was an air of uncertainty. No repairs were made to the fort; no new buildings erected. It gradually fell into a sad state of disrepair.

At the North West Company's headquarters in Montreal, too, things were not going well. Rivalry with the Hudson's Bay Company had broken into actual warfare. Both concerns were being weakened by the conflict. At last in 1821 they united, only just in time. The United States suddenly awakened to the fact that her sovereignty had been established on the Northwest Coast where her traders had operated in ships for many years. Russia, too, aroused herself and laid claim to all the land as far south from her Alaskan possessions as latitude 51 N. Spain, which had always asserted rights on the littoral and which were not clarified by the Nootka Convention of 1790, now sold her claims on all lands north of Latitude 42 to the United States, giving that country real strength behind her pretensions. It was a dark outlook for British traders.

The Foreign Office in London sent for Governor J. H. Pelly of the Hudson's Bay Company. The whole situation was surveyed. The improbability of maintaining a foothold on the south side of the Columbia was frankly admitted. The Company was advised to cross to the other side of the river and build a new fort: it might contribute to holding the river as the eventual boundary line—but it was only a hope. Something must be done—and quickly, to give Great Britain a firm foothold on the Pacific Coast.

George Simpson left York Factory on August 15 for the other side of the continent. Simpson, governor of the northern department in America for the Hudson's Bay Company, had come to the fur fields shortly before the union of the companies, and now was anxious to return to London to marry. But romance had to be put aside for the time being.

It was imperative that he cross the continent and examine the situation on the Columbia River. So, with incredible speed, the Little Emperor as he became known, travelled. He lowered the existing time for the journey between oceans by twenty days. Before leaving "the Bay" he had long talks with J. G. McTavish, who had bought Fort Astoria from the Astorians and who was now chief factor in charge of York Factory for the united companies. James McMillan was there, too. He had attained to partnership as a chief trader, and was to accompany Simpson on his long trip.

Dr. John McLoughlin, whose name was to become interwoven with the history of the west, had already left for the Columbia, where he was to take charge. He preceded Simpson by 19 days, but was overtaken before he reached the passes of the Rocky Mountains. At Jasper House, McLoughlin's Métis step-son Thomas McKay joined them.

Simpson's active mind was busy with schemes for reorganization of the whole trade of the country. Foremost of all projects he considered to be occupation of the Fraser River—where Great Britain's claim to sovereignty was strongest. It was north of latitude 49 which had been tentatively advanced in 1818 as a suitable line for an international boundary.

The dangers of the wilderness had no effect on Simpson. It was while he was shooting Death Rapids on the Big Bend of the Columbia River that he broached the subject of the Fraser River to James McMillan:

> In the course of the Day I imparted to Mr. McMillan my views in regard to extending the trade to the Northwest of Fort George and pointed out to him the importance of having an establishment at the mouth of Frazer's River; this was done with the view that he should volunteer his services to explore the Coast at length in the course of the winter, but he did not see my drift, or would not take the hint; in the evening, however, I again opened the subject and intimated that rather than allow an other Season pass without obtaining a knowledge of the Coast natives and resources of that part of the Country (our ignorance of which after being established on the Coast upwards of Fourteen years being a disgrace to the whole concern) I should undertake it myself; this had the desired effect and Mr. McMillan immediately offered his services on this dangerous and unpleasant mission.

Who would accompany McMillan as his lieutenants? They must be good men; men of courage, resource and ability to observe the country and write an intelligible report. McMillan suggested Thomas McKay; he was well versed in the habits and ways of the Indians and was active despite a stiff leg, and—as for courage—he did not know what it was to fear! Then there was a young Irishman, whom they would meet near Spokane House; McMillan had great confidence in him. His name was John Work. There was still another clerk of good education—he had formerly been a schoolteacher near Quebec—who might be suitable. He was a Métis named Francois Noel Annance. In addition to these aides, McMillan asked that the senior interpreter at Fort George, Michel Laframboise also make one of the party.

Not long after Simpson was able to confide to his journal:

> And in regard to its (the Fraser River) situation we know from Indian report that it falls into the Strait or Sound that divides Vancouver's Island from the Mainland near about Burrard's Canal or 49 to 50 North Latitude. In order however to remove all doubts I despatched Chief Trader McMillan with a party of about Forty (who would otherwise have been laying idle here all winter) a few Days after my arrival at this place, altho the Season was extremely unfavorable for such an enterprise and I entertain sanguine hopes that he will accomplish the object of his mission with credit to himself and to the satisfaction of all concerned by bringing a favorable report on the various points on which we require information and which is an essential to carrying the present plan into effect. Taking such for granted, I would establish the principal Depot at the mouth of Frasers River from whence a Vessel for China would sail annually with the returns, where the Coasting craft would receive their outfits and deliver their returns and from whence all the posts of New Caledonia, Spokan, Nez Perces, Flat Head and Coutonais also Fort George if we are allowed to occupy a Post on the Columbia.

Simpson was preparing against eventualities. He was doing what he could to retrieve the misfortune to his country of Black's pomposity and wine.

3
Through Mud and Misery

George Simpson, lord of the far-flung fur empire of the Hudson's Bay Company in North America, and Jean Ba'tiste Proveau, one of the humbler servants of the mighty organization, were happy. Thirty-nine other individuals, including Chief Factor James McMillan and three clerks, found no cause for rejoicing as they prepared to embark upon an expedition of exploration to an unknown country north of the Columbia River.

It was not that McMillan, or Thomas McKay the Fearless, or Francois Noel Annance the Learned, or John Work the indefatigable, were not interested in the purpose of the journey or that they were unduly frightened by possible dangers to be encountered. They would have welcomed the adventure in proper season, but now, in the third week of November, 1824, under raw, cold, drizzling skies, with mud underfoot, it must of necessity be a cheerless and miserable affair.

Then, too, there was grumbling at the thought of being absent from Fort George at Christmas, when it was customary to give the men a regale. They looked forward for months to the holiday season with feasting and drinking and dancing and fighting—and now they were to spend Christmas in a tractless wilderness. The officers, too, had looked forward to the Yuletide, for it was then that there was momentary relaxation from the constant strain of striving for furs, of vigilant preparation against savage treachery. This year the festive board at Fort George would be graced by Governor Simpson, who had chosen to winter on the coast. John McLoughlin would be there too. He was the new chief factor—an old gray of the Nor'west—and had come to take charge of the district, and to carve for himself a great place in the history of the Northwest. A towering man, whose very height impressed the natives, he had abandoned a career as country physician for the peril and excitement of the fur trade. Of course Chief Factor Alexander Kennedy would also be present.

In place of enjoying the society of these great men in the officers' hall on Christmas Day, McMillan and Work, Annance and McKay must, perforce, spend that occasion directing the moving of heavy boats and baggage over a difficult portage, ankle deep in mud. No wonder there was murmuring amongst the men and no gladness in the hearts of the officers as they pushed off from Fort George. Even Michel Laframboise, the interpreter, a restless soul who delighted in change and excitement, was not pleased to be sent on such an errand.

But Simpson, the pink-cheeked little governor, was delighted, with good reason. He had reached the mouth of the Columbia River but ten days before, determined that the exploration of the country in the vicinity of the Fraser's mouth should be undertaken without loss of time. Fourteen years had passed since fur traders had established themselves on the Columbia, and in that time no effort had been made to follow up the discoveries of Simon Fraser who had almost—but not quite—reached the sea. International bickering made it essential, even as the security of the Hudson's Bay Company required that the British company should occupy the banks of that muddy stream to the north.

Simpson had not been five years in America. He had come from headquarters in London, picked from a clerical position to undertake a hurried mission to the fur fields. He was to return in a few months, but winter overtook him, and he went to distant Fort Wedderburn, where he stayed. When, in 1821, the two companies merged, this little-known clerk was chosen for his loyalty and anonymity, over veterans of the fur trails to head the disrupted and disorganized affairs in the half-continent between Hudson Bay and the Pacific Coast.

Experienced men in the services of both old concerns grumbled and scoffed that a mere boy—a little boy at that—should be put over them. But Simpson amazed them. The boy had a will of cold steel, a grasp of the details of the fur trade and a determination that would tolerate neither delay nor excuses. One thing only counted—success. Then, too, although small in stature, he demonstrated that he could complete the longest trips in quicker time than could the most experienced of them.

So it was that he reduced the time for crossing the continent by 20 days and when the record was again lowered it was Simpson, himself, who did it.

Even before the completion of his breath-taking dash from the east he was planning the details of the expedition to the Fraser River, and he badgered McMillan, a travelling companion, into volunteering to head it. But McMillan had no idea that almost before he had time to recover from the fatigue of hurrying across the continent he would be on his way north. There had been no pause in Governor Simpson's insistence for immediate action. Boats were constructed and all the details of the expedition were completed within ten days.

Such activity had never been witnessed at Fort George. It had been a lethargic place, but Simpson determined to alter all that: "It is now, however, necessary that a radical change should take place and we have no time to lose in bringing it about," he noted in his diary. The change was under way. The departure of McMillan and his men was evidence of the new policy of speed and efficiency. So, Simpson was pleased.

Jean Ba'tiste Proveau was delighted. His hour had come. He had accompanied Simon Fraser on his epic journey down the great river that had since been named for the explorer. Jean Ba'tiste was never tired of telling of that trip—but his fellow engages were growing weary of hearing him boast of it. Now, with the departure of McMillan's party from Fort George he was of the number. Moreover, he had been personally interviewed by the great Governor, and by Dr. McLoughlin, and frequently by Mr. McMillan, and his advice had been solicited by these great men. He would prove to the doubters! So Jean Ba'tiste Proveau shared with Governor Simpson pleasure at the departure of the party, the trials and triumphs of which he would also share.

November 18 was a miserable day. There was a cold drizzle, that for nearly two weeks had only varied in volume. The party was not going by the easier Cowlitz Portage. They were to follow an entirely new route, known to them only by Indian report. This decision was based upon caution. Six years before, in retaliation for the killing of an Iroquois trapper, James Keith had sent Peter Skene Ogden to avenge the murder. He had done so by sudden attack upon an unsuspecting village. Thirteen had been slain.

Since that blood-soaked night the followers of the Nor'west Company and their successors had avoided the Cowlitz Portage. So McMillan was essaying with his three heavy boats, laden with supplies for 40 men for several months, to carve out a new way to the north from Baker Bay.

It was blowing hard at the mouth of the Columbia. It was impossible to round Cape Disappointment. The alternative was to portage across to Shoalwater Bay. This was a hard task. Along the shores of the bay they lined their boats in heavy wind and water—a dangerous and difficult work, for men had to try and keep the craft from dashing against the rocks, while others tugged at the lines. Entering a small stream they forced their way up through the driftwood and overhanging growth to the end of a 10-mile portage to Grays Harbor. From here, by way of the Chehalis River and a tributary named Black River, they reached Tumwater Lake, then by another portage they came to Eld Inlet on Puget Sound. It was a most exhausting journey. Chilled to the bone, the men suffered from being continually wet. Jacques Potvin, one of the voyageurs, developed blood poisoning in one of his feet. He had to be carried over the portages. At last, when it was seen that his condition was growing worse, Indians were secured to carry him back to the fort, and one of the men was detached to accompany him. There had been two accessions of the party—or more properly three—for Iroquois George, a free man, brought his slave with him. The other was Pierre Charles, a famous hunter and middleman, whose gun was to add to the food supply of the party.

It was easier travelling in the sheltered waters of Puget Sound. Now sails could be used to help the weary paddlers, but progress was made carefully and cautiously. Indian interpreters had to be recruited as different tongues were encountered. The process of gaining information became more difficult as the party advanced. Several Indians would be utilized as intermediary interpreters before a language could be understood by Laframboise.

At last the party reached a shallow bay—known today as Semiahmoo Bay—on December 11. The weather was growing colder. The wind was blowing. Ahead of them was a wide open stretch of water and the rounding of Point Roberts. They waited. But let John Work tell the story as he set it down in his journal:

> Monday 13—Embarked at half past 7 o'clock and set out with the intention of crossing the traverse, but had gone but a short way when it was thought too rough...the course was therefore changed and the boats crossed the entrance of the little bay in which we had been encamped, and continued along the main shore to another bay (Mud Bay) down which they proceeded to the entrance of a small river, (Nicomekl) up which they continued about 7 or 8 miles, in a very winding course which was in general N. Easterly. Encamped at half past 3 o'clock.

The point above mentioned to which it was intended to cross in the morning is represented by the Indians to form the entrance of the Coweechin River (which is supposed to be the same with Frasers) on the S.E. side, it projects far out to sea and appears like an island, but seems to be joined to the main land which is very low, by a muddy ridge which probably be covered at high water. Immense flocks of plover were observed flying about this sand...

The reason of proceeding up the Little River was the Indians representing that by making a portage there was a road this way into the Coweechin River, but they said it was very bad and seemed most desirous to go by the point. The Navigation of the Little River is very bad after getting a short way up it was often barred up with drift wood which impeded our progress, tho' the Indians had cut roads through it for their canoes yet they were too narrow for our boats.

Farther up it is very nearly closed up with willows so uncommonly thick that it was both laborious and tedious to get the boats dragged through them. It is yet some distance to the portage. The appearance of the country round the bay from where we started from this morning round to the point appears low, and flat the bay appears to be shallow.

In the river nothing but little willows are seen for some distance from the water where the banks, though low, are well wooded with pine, cedar, alder and some other trees. There are appearances of beaver being pretty numerous in this river. Where we are now encamped is a pretty little plain.

During the course of the day they found two Indian boys in a lodge, and gave presents to them.

The next day it was found "that the boats could proceed no farther up the river." Carrying the heavy craft was resorted to by the men. The portage was 7,910 yards in length, the careful Work noted, explaining that 3,910 yards were completed the first day. The Indians knew this portage as "T'salkwakyan," a name that they also applied to the crooked little river that led to the Fraser, and which is now known as the Salmon.

This portage...lies through a little plain which with the mighty rain has become so soft and miry that in several places it resembles a swamp...Elk have been very numerous here some time ago, but the hunters suppose that since the rainy season they have gone to the high grounds.

So the journey went on—back-breaking work, dragging the heavy boats through the mire and carrying heavy loads of baggage and supplies through knee-deep mud—but the trained observers could see that it was a pleasant land despite the miseries of the moment. At last they came to the banks of the Salmon.

It was at 1 o'clock on the afternoon of December 16 that the boats, bearing McMillan—and carrying too, Jean Ba'tiste Proveau—and their companions, emerged from the twisting, turning little stream into the broad flood of the brown Stalo. The Sky People had come again.

Now the tongue of Jean Ba'tiste was busy, for he recognized the twin peaks of T'lagunna Mountain, which white men later named Golden Ears. "Yes, that island!" He recalled passing bits of land and features of the vicinity, as the boats proceeded slowly up the river for several miles. Proveau was not mistaken; this was the river he had visited with Fraser. Even John Work, who had been a mite dubious about the story, had to admit that everything tallied with Proveau's description. It was a grand day for Jean Ba'tiste.

The party encamped about 3 p.m. and rested until 7 a.m. Before dawn they were once more on their way. They went some 18 or 20 miles up river, encamping again at the outlet from Hatzic Lake. Work relates:

> A high mountain covered with snow appeared to the S.W. in the morning, and shortly a ridge also topped with snow was seen extending from N.W. to N.E. Two peaks of this ridge are very high; as we are approaching these mountains the country is getting hilly.

> In the forepart of the day we saw an Indian lodge in a little bay on the E. side of the river. Our Indians were sent ahead to apprise the inhabitants of our approach and good intentions which prevented them from taking alarm. This was a miserable habitation formed of planks, both sides and roof; the usual appendages of Indian houses, filth and nastiness were here in abundance....Nevertheless the inmates...appeared healthy and seemed to have plenty of dry salmon provided. Our Indians were understood by these people, yet we got very little information from them.

But the following day more definite data was secured, for it was found that the natives spoke a dialect akin to the Okanagan tongue which McMillan, himself, understood. Work wrote:

> Saturday, 18th—Rained without intermission all night and all day. About 9 o'clock 47 Men, 3 Women and 1 boy of the Cohoutilt Indians (which is the name of the tribe that inhabit the village above where we were encamped) visited us, in a friendly manner. Some presents were given them consisting of a fish hook to each of 3 or 4 chiefs. A few beaver skins were also purchased from one of the chiefs for a couple of axes and a few beads. They laid no value on tobacco and would not use

it. These Indians though of the same tribe were much more intelligent than those we saw yesterday.

A new blanket, two guns, a pair of trousers, and a few other European articles, some of them very old and worn out, were in the possession of these people; these articles we understood were received in barter from tribes farther up the river, and that they had passed from white people through several tribes before that. A good deal of information was received from these people respecting the river. A letter being presented to the Chief to forward to Thompson River, he mentioned no fewer than 15 tribes...through whose hands it must pass before it reached the Forks.

The chief of this tribe is a fine tall good looking man, but his people are of low stature. Their elderly men have generally beards. All their heads are a little flattened. Their clothes consisted of blankets of their own manufacture, some white and some gray or a black brown, with varigated bands of different colors mostly red and white. They wore mats to keep off the rain, and conical hats.

On account of the short stay we could observe nothing respecting the manners, or mode of living of these people. They offered roasted sturgeon for sale which shows that these fish are in the river, but of their mode of taking them we know nothing. Our Indian guide understood them and was understood also. The language they speak has some little resemblance to the Okanagan.

Mr. McMillan having determined to return, deciding it unnecessary to proceed farther up the river past noon and returned to near the camp which we left yesterday.

The party got under way again early on the 19th and made camp that night opposite Annacis Island near the point where the Great Northern Railway now meets the Fraser River. Here they found an abandoned village, and here, too, they cut the initials, "H.B.Co" into the bark of a big tree. Henceforth it was known as H.B.Co Tree Point.

The following morning the mouth of the river was reached. Work wrote:

The channel through which we came was sounded in several places towards its discharge and found to be from 7 to 31/2 fathoms about high water. We saw a canoe with 6 Indians near the entrance to the River. On being called to by our Indians they approached to within a short distance of the boats, but could not be prevailed upon to come nearer.

31

So it was that Simon Fraser's great work was completed, and the river's mouth was found. It had required 32 days for the journey from Fort George. Now, however, with the vision of the comforts of home before them and spurred on by the possibility of being in time for the New Year's regale, the men worked with renewed energy at the paddles and tugged and pulled and carried with added strength over the portages. McMillan and his men reached the Columbia as the old year closed.

Governor George Simpson smiled happily as he greeted the return of the explorers. He bestowed praise generously. Jean Ba'tiste Proveau threw out his chest and claimed his full measure of it.

There remained one thing upon which Simpson and McLoughlin required information: what was the depth of the channel over the bar at the mouth of the Fraser. McLoughlin promised he would obtain precise information during the summer.

In August the ship *William and Ann* arrived from England. McLoughlin made arrangements for her to go to the mouth of the Fraser. Alexander McKenzie, a promising clerk, and J. P. Swan, chief officer of the vessel, were charged with making a survey of the river entrance.

It was McKenzie's first glimpse of the Fraser; it would have been better for him had he never set eyes upon it.

Governor Simpson was able to inform London that there were no obstacles to navigation of the river from the sea. There was sufficient depth of water to float the *William and Ann* across the bar.

The Governor and Committee in London, having considered all the reports wrote, February 23, 1826:

> We wish Frasers River to be established next season if possible, and Mr. McMillan should be appointed to the charge of it, as his reappearance among the natives may have a good effect. From the central situation of Frasers River we think it probable that it will be found to be the proper place for the principal depot, but not until we have passed at least one winter there, and acquired a knowledge of the character and disposition of the Natives and ascertained whether the navigation of the River is favorable to the Plan of making it the principal communication with the Interior.

Occupation of the coast, north of the 49th parallel, was approaching. The shadow of the Union Jack was spreading over the muddy waters of the second great river of the west.

4

Civilization and Savagery

Whattlekainum heard exciting rumors of a vessel trying to enter the muddy mouth of the Stalo. He heard of the great white-winged canoes of the white-faced strangers, whom he had first encountered on the river 19 years ago. Since that time he had been told by visiting Clallam, Saanich and Songhee of the great canoes in which the *Whan-ee-tum*, as they were called, came to trade such fascinating things for furs.

There was a time when Whattlekainum had believed that the *Whan-ee-tum* were supernatural, that they came from the sky. That was when Simon Fraser arrived from the interior, and Whattlekainum saved his life and those of his companions. Whattlekainum was glad now that he had done do. He wanted to be friendly with such interesting people.

So Whattlekainum started off down the river to see who the strangers might be. Perhaps it would be the same chief who had come during the rains of two winters ago! "There was a great canoe." It was just as the men from the sea coast had described. Her wings were folded. She was riding at anchor in the river between what the whites now call Annacis Island and the southern shore of the river.

Cautiously Whattlekainum approached. He was invited to come aboard. He did so, and met the great chief called McMillan. Whattlekainum was delighted, but he stayed only a few moments. He must hurry to tell his people that old friends had returned to the Stalo.

Upriver, taking advantage of the eddies in order to make all haste, Whattlekainum paddled. He stopped to tell old Punnis, an irascible chief at Kikait, of the approach of the schooner. Punnis did not welcome the tidings. He recalled those days of long ago when Fraser had kicked the young men who stole from his packs. He remembered, too, how that insult could have been wiped out in accordance with the blood-code of the coast, had it not been for the interference of Whattlekainum. Now Whattlekainum wanted to greet these strangers once more as friends. Old Punnis would have none of it.

The *Cadboro*, Captain Aemilius Simpson, a man both punctilious and eccentric, slowly made her way against the current. The vessel was bringing James McMillan, now a chief factor, who had headed the winter expedition of 1824, to discover the mouth of the river and examine its lower reaches for an eligible site for a fort, with a party to carry out that objective. With him was Francois Noel Annance, the Métis scholar who delighted in contemplating the classics amid the dangers and privations of the wooded wilderness of the west. There were two other clerks, Donald Manson and George Barnston, and some twenty-five men. A strong fort was to be erected—that is a defensive work that would hold against the arrows and spears of savages, but which would offer little, if any, resistance to artillery.

The *Cadboro* emerged from the channel into the wider portion of the river and edged on past Kikait. Now was the moment that Punnis had anticipated. He gave a signal and out from hiding swept 150 braves in their war canoes—only to stop and gape in amazement at the huge canoe, larger by many times than those of the Yuculta. In vain Punnis screamed orders to rush the schooner, but his army was overpowered by awe and curiosity. No one moved.

Aboard the *Cadboro*, as soon as the Indians appeared, loaded cannons were trained on the frail craft. Muskets and sabres were served out to the sailors, and muskets to the passengers. Captain Simpson donned a new pair of white kid gloves—as was his custom in moments of danger. All the while the schooner kept her way upriver and round the Slikwhinna—or Big Horn, as the Indians knew the great bend. All the while Old Punnis screamed himself black in the face without doing the slightest injury to the schooner.

The *Cadboro* had been off the river's mouth some days. In addition to the officers and men charged with the duty of establishing civilization on the banks of the Fraser within the picketted few acres of a post to be called Fort Langley—in honor of Thomas Langley, an aging director of the Hudson's Bay Company—there were two distinguished native guests. Chief Scanawa had come with McMillan from the Cowlitz Portage to Puget Sound and had there boarded the schooner. He would be a useful man to assure communications with Fort Vancouver on the Columbia, the larger establishment that superseded Fort George.

The other native to share honors and attention with Scanawa was Shashia, king of the Cowichan. He was the most influential of all the chiefs of that great confederacy, enjoying a measure of authority in other sub-tribes as well as in that of the Cowichan—Halkomelem—proper on Vancouver Island. Shashia quitted the vessel when it entered the river, to rejoin it later.

As the schooner made slow way upstream, McMillan and his men scrutinized the shores carefully. They were nearing the little river from which, two and a half years before—in 1824—they had entered the Fraser. This appeared a suitable site, and the chief factor and one of his clerks went ashore to examine it carefully. It might do, unless there was a better location higher up.

The following morning, July 27, 1827, it was recorded in McMillan's journal:

> Mr. McMillan accompanied by Mr. McLeod and Mr. Annance and Shashia, went off up the river to look for a more eligible situation for an establishment.

They found what appeared to be a most desirable spot, and next day all hands were employed warping the schooner upstream to that place. It was found, however, that the *Cadboro* could not come within 300 yards of the site. This would not do, for it was imperative that cargoes should be unloaded and freights taken on from a wharf, while during building operations the vessel must be moored close enough to give protection to the shore party.

There was only one thing to do. It was to drop down river again to the place that had first attracted their attention. So it was that actual occupation of the soil of the Fraser fan was commenced on Monday, July 30. The weather was fine, and, according to the journal:

> The schooner was brought close to the shore and the horses landed by slinging them off to the bank. The poor animals appeared to rejoice heartily in their liberation. Our men at noon were all busily employed clearing the ground for the establishment. In the evening all came on board to sleep, a precaution considered necessary until we are better assured of the friendly disposition of the natives. A few Indians and Indian women were alongside for a great part of the day, and were quiet and peaceable. One of the ship's company was this day put in irons for making use of language calculated to promote discontent and create disorder amongst the crew.

At five the following morning the laborers were landed to renew their struggle with the forest. The site selected was covered with big trees, the underbrush heavy and tangled. Indians crowded about to watch the *Whan-ee-tum*. This was work for squaws, not for warriors, they thought; but, there might be opportunity of pilfering some of the magnificent tools that these strangers used.

In this, at least, one of the natives was successful, for next morning it was found that an axe was missing. The culprit, an old man, was detected and made to surrender it. For a time it was feared that trouble might ensue. Between 40 and 50 Indians assembled. They all talked excitedly, waved their arms and milled about, while several chiefs harangued them, "the purport of which was upon the whole of a friendly character."

The weather was hot, but the men were not permitted to take long periods of rest. The work to be accomplished was too vital. So, with perspiration running down their faces French Canadians, Sandwich Islanders, Americans, Englishmen and Iroquois toiled at the cutting of pickets for palisades; squaring of timbers for bastions, and the making of lumber for houses and stores, as well as the torturous labor of clearing land. From break of day until after dark they toiled, while round them hovered savages whose interest was, to say the least, open to suspicion. Shashia reported that amongst the Indians there was a feeling that the *Whan-ee-tum* should not be allowed to settle.

Now the first suggestion of hostility tightened up the discipline of the men, and aroused all to tense watchfulness. The Indians set fire to the forest in an effort to drive the fort builders away. The men cutting pickets had to run from the flames. The fire burned fiercely all next day, August 11. The incendiary endeavor only served to speed up efforts to complete at least one of the bastions, so that protection should be available. By nightfall of that day it was so far advanced that the journalist commented: "It appears to command respect." By the evening of August 13 it only required a roof of bark to complete it. Pierre Charles was one of those detailed to obtain bark.

Soon the bastion was finished. Artillery could now be put in it, and men could shelter there in need. The work of hacking down trees, squaring timbers and cutting pickets went on apace as expert French-Canadian axmen demonstrated their ability with the broadaxe.

By August 20 the picketting was cut, and digging of a trench three feet deep around what was to be the area of the fort was commenced. By the end of the month the second bastion was finished, and erection of the palisades started.

Now the weather, which had been excellent, changed. It started to rain. This, however, was not permitted to slow down operations; witness:

> Sunday, September 2—It being a most desirable object to have an inclosure up as quickly as possible, all hands with the exception of the sick and maimed are at work. No Indians were allowed to land, on account of the theft committed yesterday (when some few articles were stolen) but the want of fresh provisions will soon compel us to concede a little in regard to this restriction.

In fact the order was relaxed a little that very night, for the great Shashia arrived and was permitted to camp alongside the uncompleted fort.

One by one men sickened, and after a week of rain, hope was expressed in the journal that there would soon be improvement in the weather:

> For the sake of advance with our business, as well as the health of the people, who have not yet had time to put up for themselves anything like comfortable lodgings, and consequently suffer much from their constant exposure to so wet a climate. Sickness at present prevails among them to an alarming extent, and we can ascribe it only to this, and the change of their diet. They are now living entirely upon fish, whereas their rations before consisted chiefly of grain—say Indian corn, pease and c...

These sick, weary men had before them constant reminders of the dangerous country to which they had come. On September 7 it was noted:

> A Clallam woman, sister-in-law of Scanawa, has been restored by the Yucultas who had taken her prisoner in their last plundering excursion. Her ransom has cost Scanawa seven or eight blankets, besides other trifling articles of trade. The negotiator was a Yuculta woman who is married to an Indian that lives up this river and is well known here by the name of The Doctor.

But the success of The Doctor on behalf of Scanawa proved to be fatal to her. Another Indian, who had relatives held by the northern raiders, was so enraged over her failure to liberate them as well that he killed her.

Soon the fort builders could breathe easier. On September 8:

> Picketting of the fort was completed and the gates hung. The rectangle inside is 40 yds. by 45; the two bastions 12 ft. square

> each, built of 8-inch logs and having a lower and upper floor-
> ing, the latter of which is to be occupied by our artillery. The
> tout ensemble must have a formidable enough appearance to
> the eyes of the Indians, especially those here who have seen
> nothing of the kind before.

Here, on this enclosed ground of little more than half an acre, British civilization on the Pacific Coast was planted.

A week later the first storehouse was "roofed in with an excellent bark covering." Immediately work commenced transferring stores and equipment from the schooner to shore. Then ballast was taken in, Captain Simpson, who had been charting the river during the long weeks that the schooner was idle, was anxious to get away. He was to cruise around the Strait of Georgia trading for skins where such could be done advantageously, and notifying Indians of the establishment of the trading post on the Fraser River. On the morning of September 18 the schooner weighed and saluted the fort with three guns. From the bastions three guns were fired in return compliment: the *Cadboro* swung slowly around and headed down stream for the sea. Fort Langley was left to its own devices.

Now Indians came in crowds to see what McMillan and his men were doing. They came from Vancouver Island; overland from Cowlitz Portage; from the Howe Sound villages of the Squamish, and from Burrard Inlet. Clallam from the south side of the Strait of Juan de Fuca came to spy and pry and to barter over prices.

"These Indians," McMillan declared, "make great difficulty in bartering with us at our prices, on account of having been visited by the Americans last Spring, who supplied them with goods more cheaply than we do."

Competition of the Boston traders was already felt and would be for a long time.

Hardly had the Hudson's Bay men become established behind the rough pickets of Fort Langley than they witnessed the ferocity of the wilds. A war party of Cowichan, accompanied by some Nanaimo, stole up the river to make a surprise attack on the Chilliwack in retaliation for some real or fancied grievance. After several scouting parties had inspected the locality, the raid was carried out.

"The war party of Cowichans returned this afternoon," says the journal. "They have murdered one man and a woman and taken several women and children prisoners, who, as a matter of course, become slaves. The head of one of their victims was pendant at the bow of one of the canoes, presenting a spectacle as dismal and disgusting as can well be imagined; a spectacle the most shocking to humanity that this land of savage barbarism produces. The greater number of the canoes were laden with dried and fresh provisions, baskets, mats and other furnishings, the spoils of the camp of the unhappy creatures that they had surprised."

By September 26 it was noted that "the wintering house" was close to completion, and men were working hard in an endeavor to finish it. It was 30 feet in length by 15 in width, divided into two apartments, with a fireplace and two windows in each.

Now the great migration of Indians from above was in full swing. These Indians who had gathered from far and near to catch salmon were on their way home, but before taking final departure from the river would stop at Saan-a-sant—or Pitt River—to dig *skous*—the white man's arrow-head—a tuber that grows in pools and swamps, and which was considered a delicacy. Here as many as 5,000 Indians would assemble. Harvesting of the root, dances and feasting and quarrelling would occupy them. Here new feuds often started.

As watchers on the stockades saw canoes by the hundred pass down the river, a sense of loneliness was impressed upon the miserable men who, wet to the skin and chilled to the bone by the first cold of approaching winter, exclaimed, "Even the Indians quit this desolate land." On October 7, two Indians, strangers, came down river bearing a letter from Archibald McDonald at Fort Kamloops. Here, then, was evidence that communication could be had with the far Interior—but the letter was dated in October of the previous year.

Now, by Chakeinook, chief of a band of Saanich Indians who was encamped at the end of the portage, came disquieting rumors. He had heard, he said, that the Yuculta had cut off a boat's crew from the *Cadboro*; and then, too, he announced that the same fearful warriors planned a retaliatory raid on the Stalo people because of the murder of The Doctor. There might be no truth in the story of the attack on *Cadboro's* men, but that the Yuculta planned mischief for the death of the woman was plausible; it was in keeping with the coastal blood-code.

Later, the little garrison at Fort Langley was to learn that the report of the murderous surprise attack on *Cadboro's* crew was only too true. The schooner had been up the narrows as far as Salmon River and was returning. Near the present site of Comox a boat was sent ashore to the mouth of a small creek to fill water casks. Indians gathered about, apparently upon terms of friendship. Suddenly a sailor named Driver was seized from behind and his musket was wrenched from his grasp. He was killed.

Another white, a boy named Peter Calder, was wounded in the ensuing struggle. Relief came from the schooner, and the Indians were driven away. Then the *Cadboro* sailed away. Whether or not Captain

Simpson was in a position to exact vengeance is not clear, but white men had been killed and the murderers had escaped. The result was to bring all whites into contempt: "These men who do the work of women have hearts of squaws: they do not fight."

These were gloomy days, and dreary nights. The shortening, wet, cheerless days, the ration of dried fish and venison and the illness that attacked the men were bad for morale. McMillan seized upon the advent of All Saint' Day, November 1, as an excuse for a regale. Rum was measured out generously; additional food supplies from the treasured stock in the storeroom, grain and peas, were given, and laughter and song were heard for the first time in many weeks.

Rain, rain, rain—only varied in its volume; cold, increasing cold; that was the daily ration of weather. There were muddy pools everywhere. The horses had been so weak when landed that they could hardly stand. They had but little chance to gain strength since, for they had, of necessity, to be worked hard. One was caught in a quagmire and perished. A few days later another was drowned in flood waters in a nearby creek.

Everything appeared to be ominous. Even nature grumbled and threatened. On November 23, it was recorded:

> Last night a noise was heard by some of the men, resembling the sound of distant cannon. The houses were shaken a little at the time, which makes us suppose that it was a slight shock of earthquake, as a tree falling would not have been so readily felt.

Through all the dreary days the men had toiled unremittingly, and now, November 26, there was another celebration in recognition of their faithful endeavors.

> This morning a flag staff was cut and prepared and in the afternoon erected in the South East corner of the Fort. The usual forms were gone through. Mr. Annance officiated in baptising the establishment, and the men were regaled in celebration of the event. Our two hunters came home at night, having been alarmed at the firing which took place on the occasion.

So it was that after years of planning, and months of backbreaking toil amid ever-present dangers, that Fort Langley was established under the "H.B.CO"—initialled red ensign of Great Britain, on the banks of the great river that Simon Fraser had explored.

5

Merriment and Murder

"Dull and monotonous—everything has a wintery appearance," was the entry in the Fort Langley journal for December 8, 1827. The aspect was indeed cheerless; leafless deciduous trees and dark, gloomy conifers loomed across the Fraser River; a sprinkling of snow, dull grey skies, chilly days and cold nights; all these depressed the spirits of the pioneers.

Men shivered as they toiled, cutting and squaring timber for additional buildings or rough-hewing battens for lining the stockades. Heavy work it was at any time, it was now, since the horses brought from the Columbia had perished in the clammy quagmires of autumn, the labor of beasts added to the normal toil of man. They had to pull and drag and strain to get the heavy timbers home.

Approach of the year-end holidays brought no comfort. They accentuated the loneliness and desolation of that first winter on the Fraser, by contrast with other posts and happier Yuletides spent elsewhere. So December dragged on. Men cursed and grew bitter, but they could do nothing about it. McMillan and the clerks suffered as much as the laborers. There was warmth within the houses, and a sufficiency of dried salmon, with an occasional treat of venison. It was the isolation and dull monotony of a comfortless country that bore down on all.

Now it was Christmas Eve. Men muttered as they listlessly gathered fire-wood for the morrow. The river was frozen over and the snow was deeper. The muffled guards on the galleries stamped their feet and swung their arms to quicken the blood as they scanned the dull white waste before them.

Suddenly one of the men stiffened and peered down river. Then he called the attention of his companion to a movement among the trees. Soon the object of their scrutiny could be seen more clearly. It was an Indian, and he was hurrying. Indians did not usually hasten on foot. The native was making no attempt to conceal himself from the guards. Now he was out on the ice. As he came closer they could see that he was waving something. It was a note.

"Quick!" shouted McMillan, when the missive had been brought to him. "Quick, sound the alarm! Mr. McKenzie, from Fort Vancouver, and four men are dangerously situated among the Musqueam at the Kwantlen River."

In a few minutes an armed party, headed by Donald Manson and Francois Annance was on its way down river to the rescue of Alexander McKenzie, chief trader in the Hudson's Bay Company's service, and his men. They had gone only a few miles when they met McKenzie. Ice had compelled them to land amongst the Musqueam, who were camped at the junction of the two rivers. There they had been threatened and robbed, but the chief trader had induced a Kwantlen to carry the message to the fort.

There was great rejoicing when the visitors to the fort were welcomed by beaming James McMillan. McKenzie's men were given boisterous greetings by Jean Ba'tiste and Louis and the others. Gloom vanished by magic. Was there ever a more glorious surprise? Here were friends who had come all the dangerous and uncomfortable way from the Columbia River to bring them Christmas mail and good cheer.

No longer were they the forgotten men of the service. That night fire places blazed high. Laughter and violin music echoed through the fort. Even the men doing guard duty on the galleries felt warmer and more cheerful despite the weather.

What a wonderful Christmas it was! The men had a grand regale. True, there was not much variation in the generous food ration, for dried salmon was the main portion because Pierre Charles had cut his hand and could not hunt. But on the day after Christmas the huntsman insisted that he would go in search of venison for a New Year's feast. Injury or no, he would see that there would be plenty.

While Pierre Charles and his men were in the woods, Annance with a strongly armed party went to the Musqueam village to recover the property stolen from McKenzie. This was easily accomplished, for Annance had a determined way about him that the Indians recognized.

New Year's Day—an anniversary always celebrated in the fur trade with even greater enthusiasm that Christmas Day—was a joyous affair. The men called at the officers' quarters early in the morning to wish them well, and received a glass of wine and cake. Then they were each given a generous portion of venison—for Pierre Charles had done magnificently. A small amount of flour and dried peas were added to the food ration. A full pint of potent rum was ladled out to each. Men danced and shouted and fought and sang. One competed with another in feats of strength and dexterity. Next day the celebration continued.

When the merry mood was spent, McKenzie prepared to return to Fort Vancouver, James McMillan decided to accompany him. The first returns of Fort Langley were ready for presentation, McMillan was just a little proud of the fact that in addition to erecting the post he had succeeded in trading 1,182 skins, of which 683 were large beaver, 228 were small ones. Also 269 land otter had been secured by barter. It was a creditable showing.

On the morning of January 3 the party got under way. It was intended to camp at the mouth of the river. McKenzie knew the locality well. He had made soundings there in 1825, while McMillan it was who first discovered the outlet of the great, muddy stream. The guns of the fort fired a parting salute and the men gave three cheers, and then they turned again to the routine of the establishment.

Ten days later McMillan returned. The party had been stormbound at Point Roberts for a week, so he decided to defer sending the returns until later. With the men who were to accompany him to the Columbia River he came back. McKenzie went on—to his death.

Chief Scanawa, who had followed McMillan from Cowlitz Portage, had established himself beside the fort. He was becoming a man of some wealth and importance, according to Indian standards. The white men had developed a strong liking for the chief, who had appointed himself a sort of intermediary between some of the tribes and the traders, thus making himself useful to the white men and winning the enmity of local tribesmen. McMillan referred to him as his friend, and occasionally dubbed him, "a great rascal."

But all the Indian chiefs visiting Fort Langley were not opposed to Scanawa. Shashia was his friend. It was this Cowichan who brought dire intelligence to Scanawa's tent and it was passed on to McMillan.

McKenzie and his party had been wiped out, murdered by the Clallam as they camped on the shores of Puget Sound.

Now, McMillan blamed himself for not having accompanied McKenzie, but perhaps it was not as bad as the Indians said. Indians were great liars. But the report of the attack on the *Cadboro's* boat had been true. So doubts and fears haunted the minds of the chief factor and his clerks.

The news came just as preparations were being made to send Manson to Fort Vancouver with the returns. Perhaps it would be advisable to defer the expedition until more definite word was received about the fate of McKenzie: but Manson was not afraid. On February 15 he left the fort, quietly. There was no firing of salutes this time.

And now the Indians, emboldened by the massacre on Puget Sound, started a war of nerves against the little garrison of Fort Langley. A Sechelt arrived with a story that the Yuculta were preparing to come and kill the whites and take away their store of blankets.

"As this is a cheap way of getting goods," snorted McMillan, "we will not likely come to terms amicably. Our iron interpreters will have to settle the dispute."

Whattlekainum, McMillan's friend, now brought confirmatory details of the murder of McKenzie and his men.

With the opening of spring, a war party of 150 Cowichan passed up the river to raid the Chilliwack. "Ugly looking devils," muttered McMillan, as he counted the warriors. They killed 10 men and took 20 women and children prisoners.

Kennedy and Sauve, guards on the galleries, one night saw or heard—it was a dark night—Indians prowling about the fort. They challenged, and instantly came a shower of stones.

When news of the casualties amongst the Chilliwack reached him, McMillan exclaimed,

> "This warfare keeps the Indians of this vicinity in such continual alarm that they can not turn their attention to anything but the care of their families, and that they do but poorly. While the powerful tribes from Vancouver's Island harass them in this manner, little hunting can be expected from them. Unless the company supports them against those lawless villains little exertion can be expected from them."

McMillan's nerves were wearing.

A few days after this impatient outburst, Scanawa burst in to the fort, shouting that the Yuculta were coming. The alarm was sounded. Men dropped their tasks and ran to their stations. Those working in the woods dashed for the protection of the fort, while men on the galleries covered their coming. It was not the dreaded northerners who had frightened Scanawa, but a party of Indians from the Thompson River.

Such alarms became daily occurrences. McMillan almost wished that the Yuculta would make an appearance. He was worrying too, about Manson's absence.

An attempt was made upon the life of Scanawa. Sentinels saw a canoe steal quietly up the river and disembark a number of men, who crept stealthily into Scanawa's lodge near the fort. But the chief, who had a premonition of an attack about to be made, had begged his friend McMillan to permit him to sleep in the fort. But the incident decided the chief that he had better return to the Cowlitz.

Mr. Annance one evening heard noises down the river. The Yuculta were reported to be attacking the Musqueam village at the entrance to the North Arm of the Fraser. Perhaps the enemy had come! He drifted down stream in the shadow of the bank until he could hear men talking. They were strangers. Next morning with an armed party, he made a reconnaissance and found evidence that a large number of men had been sheltering in the woods. Whether or not they were Yuculta, he could not say, but the possibility was alarming.

Men kept close to the fort now. They were living under terrific strain, and McMillan was alarmed about Manson's long absence. On April 8 he confided his fears to the journal:

"I am beginning to despair of the people who went to Fort Vancouver," he wrote. But a week later Manson appeared. He had come in the *Cadboro* to the mouth of the river and continued to Fort Langley by small boat.

The joy of welcoming him was tempered by the final assurance he brought that Alexander McKenzie had perished. There had still been the faintest hope.

The *Cadboro* made her way up to the fort to unload supplies. It was a welcome break, indeed, to have Captain Simpson, his officers and men at the post for a few days, and to get news of other places and of friends. When the schooner sailed on April 21, George Barnston, a clerk, went with her, being transferred elsewhere.

Scanawa had returned. It was too dangerous for him to continue his journey.

On May 7 there was another cry raised of invasion by the Yuculta. According to the journal, "immediately all the women and children embarked in their canoes and went up the little river and hid themselves in the woods. The men made a show of remaining at the camp, or rather on the skirts of the wood. Anyone unacquainted with the Indian life would imagine all the furies of the infernal region were let loose at once; however, once the women and children and dogs were off, things got quieter."

It was on Sunday, May 11, Scanawa again made his departure. McMillan set down: "Our friend Scanawa preparing to be off for the second time; he is only waiting for the darkness of the night, when the Indians give up fishing. I wrote to Chief Factor McLoughlin by him."

Less than a week later, news seeped into Fort Langley that Scanawa was dead. He, his wife, sons and slaves—all except a Yuculta slave, for his murderers were too frightened of the vengeance of that tribe to kill him—had been murdered at Point Roberts. A wealthy Indian was Scanawa, for he had with him at the time of his death, 32 blankets, a gun, kettle, traps, axes, capots, shirts and other articles of trade goods.

The killing of Scanawa, the friend of the white man, only accentuated the dangers of the country and added force to the frequent, almost daily, reports that the Yuculta or the Kwakiutl, or even the Cowichan, were intending to raid the place. And around the very gates of the fort the fights and squabbles of local tribes swirled. Hundreds of Indians hung about the palisades.

Despite the constant strain of living amongst savages who were becoming contemptuous of the whites—because the killing of Driver, the wounding of Calder, up coast on Vancouver Island's east coast, and now the butchering of McKenzie's party and the death of Scanawa had not been revenged—the men of Fort Langley maintained a bold demeanor and went about their accustomed tasks.

But such a lesson as the tribes of Puget Sound and the Strait of Georgia would not soon forget was being prepared for them.

It was on July 15. The brigade from Fort St. James on Stuart Lake, the able-bodied from Fort Langley, the men from the Snake County, and the crew of the *Cadboro* were assembled with the retainers of Fort Vancouver in the square at that place. Dr. John McLoughlin, the gigantic, stern-visaged chief of the Hudson's Bay Company's operations west of the Rockies, spoke from the steps of the hall. He told of the murder of McKenzie, of the growing insolence of the Indians of Puget Sound and pointed out that unless there were reprisals it would not be safe for any white man to go beyond the immediate locality of a fort. He did not call for volunteers.

He did not need to call. All were ready to go. These men of the woods and rivers, French-Canadians, Iroquois from the east, Hawaiians, Scots, Americans and Chinook slaves, all were aware of the terrors of Indian warfare, but there were no slackers amongst them.

Chief Trader Alexander Roderick McLeod was selected to head the punitive expedition. Actual direction of the party was entrusted to Michel Laframboise, the restless interpreter. Clerks Thomas Dears and Frank Ermatinger, from the Columbia were assigned to the party and James Murray Yale ("Little Yale," he was called by reason of his small stature) from Fort St. James was also taken. Yale was an experienced man. He knew Indian ways and he, too, had narrowly escaped death when, several years before, his men at Fort George on the upper Fraser, were murdered during his absence. Yale was destined to play an important part in the future development of Fort Langley. Now he was going to help to make the road between that place and the Columbia River safe for white men to travel.

Some sixty men were selected for the mission. They were to go by land, while the *Cadboro* was to proceed to the Clallam country by sea. On the eve of departure the Iroquois, the Hawaiians and Chinooks, held a war dance; their painted faces and wild gestures, characteristic of their different races, silhouetted against the light from the open door of the Hall, were weirdly barbaric.

They went by way of the Cowlitz Portage, making their way slowly towards Puget Sound. On the way they encountered an Indian bearing a note addressed to Dr. McLoughlin. It was from James McMillan, the one he had entrusted to Scanawa to deliver. The murderers had sold it to a chief of a neutral tribe. He in turn had passed it on, and from village to village it had been transferred, until the messenger who brought it to McLeod sold it to the white men. Old Scanawa was known to Laframboise and others of the expedition. Word of the manner of his death made the members of the party more anxious to come to grips with the killers.

Reaching the salt water, the expedition secured canoes and headed up for the point of rendezvous with the *Cadboro*. On the way they met several Puyallup, from whom they learned that some Clallam were encamped not far from them at the beginning of a portage to Port Townsend. It was just breaking day when some of the party, headed by Ermatinger and Yale, silently crept close to the lodge where the Clallam slept. An Indian heard them. He rose and stepped to the door of the hut, only to crumple as several shots rang out. Now firing became general. When the smoke of battle cleared there were eight dead Clallam, including women and children. Two families had been wiped out.

Contact was made with the schooner, and the *Cadboro* moved on with the volunteers to Kantai at Port Townsend. The big village here was deserted. The Clallam had gone to New Dungeness where they proposed to make a stand.

When McKenzie was killed, a woman who was with the party was captured by the Clallam. She was being held prisoner and it was determined to save her life if possible. So when the schooner dropped anchor off New Dungeness, a demand was made for her liberation. This was promised, but the promise was not kept.

Several days were spent in futile negotiations. Captain Simpson and McLeod lost patience when the Clallam tried to trap them into coming ashore to attend a council meeting, where it was intended to murder them. The two Indians who brought the invitation were fired upon. One was killed, the other wounded.

Then the *Cadboro* was swung around so her guns bore upon the village. McLeod and his warriors in boats and canoes started for the beach. The cannon roared. Flimsy cedar houses splintered and collapsed. Men raced up the beach as the guns from the schooner raked the forest ahead with grape shot. The torch was applied to the remaining huts and debris, and soon the village of the Clallam was a sea of flames. Then some forty canoes drawn up on the beach were destroyed. It was learned later that about seventeen Indians had been killed.

The whites and their allies withdrew to the schooner. Several days later the woman was surrendered. Then the schooner went back to Port Townsend, and that place was also given over to the flames.

The *Cadboro* then went on to Fort Langley, and all the Indians encountered on the trip to and up the Fraser were told of what had happened to the Clallam.

McKenzie had been avenged, and Scanawa's death as well, but of greater value than vengeance was the fact that all the natives of the Inside Passage knew that the whites were not as squaws, afraid to fight. The road to Fort Langley was safe.

6

Potatoes and Fish

There was excited fluttering among the women of Fort Langley. One of the eleven members of the sex was doing something entirely feminine on the morning of July 2, 1828. She was presenting her husband with a son. Often these women, who brought the joys of domesticity to the place, squabbled and fought and scratched each other to such an extent as to receive notice of their conduct in the journal of the establishment. But not so today; it was all too important for that.

James McMillan was very interested in the happening. He realized that it was a momentous event, and he registered the birth as being the first "amongst the white," saying, that by reason of the fact, the baby would be named Louis Langley. Unfortunately the chief factor was not accustomed to the compilation of vital statistics; he neglected to give the names of the parents.

The aristocracy of female society—those women who had come with their husbands from the Columbia River—and their sisters from the delta of the Fraser chuckled and chortled and cooed and whispered and praised the infant. Jean Ba'tiste allowed, "She's fine boy, dat babee, by Gar!" Old Whattlekainum and the great Shashia came to the fort to see the tiny product of the mingling of white and red blood, and grunted their approval. Chiefs and warriors could not demonstrate their enthusiasm in such matters as did the women. Everyone was pleased at the coming of Louis Langley. It was regarded as a good omen; the white man had come to stay.

James McMillan kept his men steadily employed. There was much to be done. More buildings were required. Already the enclosed space was becoming crowded. There were gardens to be planted and culti- vated, for foodstuffs must be produced locally. Salmon had to be traded and cured for winter use. Above all, there must be a keen eye maintained upon the trade in furs. Those pestiferous Boston pedlars who came from New England in little ships and traded up and down the outer coast, occasionally venturing into the Strait of Juan de Fuca, provided compe- tition that it was hard to meet. This had been especially so before the Cla- llam had felt the fury of the white man's wrath.

After that unfortunate, but necessary, affair there was less boasting that this or that tribe was planning to destroy the fort. But always there was the threat that the Yuculta would do so. It was a tedious time, a period of unremitting toil. As summer passed and the crisp air of early October told of the approach of the white bitterness of winter men recalled the cold and misery of the frozen months that they had spent in the half completed buildings during the previous season.

Things were better now. The dwellings were snug and warm. There had been a great improvement in food, for gardens had added vegeta- bles to the daily diet. There were chickens to provide occasional eggs and it was reported that cows would soon arrive from the Columbia. It was even hinted that butter would be made. Fresh salmon were plenti- ful, while sturgeon—hideous looking fish, weighing hundreds of pounds—were offered for sale by Indians almost daily. The royal fish of Europe was common fare to the men of Fort Langley.

McMillan was tiring. He was longing for a furlough, and was won- dering if he would obtain it that year. He was entitled to a holiday. He had not heard what had been decided by the Governor and Council at the annual meeting in the east. No word of the arrangements made there in June had yet reached remote Fort Langley. Then, it was just about dusk on October 10, strange musical sounds floated down the river. Old Whattlekainum was one of the first to hear them: "Yes—it must be!" He could not mistake. It was the sound made so long ago by the Sky People, when the man blew on the head of a crane!

The skirl of the bagpipes ceased with a long, wailing note, and the singing of men grew stronger on the evening air. Ah, now there was excitement on the galleries and outside the gate on the river bank. The tune was a familiar Canadian boat song, sung with gusto by many men. It was picked up by those at the fort.

But who could these strangers be? That they were of the C(
was certain. Could it be possible that they had come all the way m.
Thompson River, or had a new route from Puget Sound to the Fraser
been discovered?

The fleet of canoes now emerged from semi-darkness and swept to
a magnificent landing at the little wharf. Out of the leading craft stepped
the small, but dignified figure of a man of importance. McMillan knew
him instantly. It was Governor Simpson himself; with him came Dr.
Richard J. Hamlyn and two men who were to play important roles in the
future development of Fort Langley: Archibald McDonald and James
Murray Yale.

Now all was excitement indeed. Such laughter and shouting and
bustling about and running hither and thither to assist in unloading the
baggage, such swaggering on the part of be-sashed and be-ribboned
voyageurs who manned the Governor's own canoe—the most expert in
the service. Such a happy night had never been seen in Fort Langley, not
even when McKenzie had arrived so unexpectedly last Christmas Eve.
Before the visitors went to bed it was decided that McMillan would join
the Governor and McDonald would remain in charge, with Yale as his
second in command, while Annance would stay as Indian trader. Manson was required elsewhere.

McDonald had been in charge of Fort Kamloops from 1826 to 1827.
A sturdy, energetic man of decision was Archibald McDonald. He was
well educated and had been a secretary to Lord Selkirk at Red River in
the days before the Union. Since that time he had served with distinction
on both sides of the mountains. In 1828 he was commissioned a chief
trader.

James Murray Yale, his health now improved, had lately taken part
in the chastisement of the Clallam. He had served the Hudson's Bay
Company since 1815. His had been a hard life. He had pioneered in the
Peace River area. He had been taken prisoner by the Nor'westers in the
days of the trade war, had narrowly escaped death at Fort George when
his men were murdered, and had served at Fort St. James. Now he had
arrived at his last station, for he was to remain at Fort Langley until his
retirement. Simpson was very fond of "Little Yale." "He is a young gen-
tleman in whom we can repose the utmost confidence," the Governor
declared.

McDonald has left his impression of Fort Langley as he first saw it:

> The fort is 135 feet by 120, with two good bastions and a gal-
> lery four feet wide all round. A building of three compart-
> ments for the men, a small log house of two compartments in
> which the gentlemen now reside, and a store are now occu-
> pied, besides which there are two other buildings, one a good

> dwelling house, with an excellent cellar and a spacious garret,
> a couple of well finished chimneys are up and the whole now
> ready for wainscotting and partitions, four large windows in
> front, one in each end and one with a corresponding door in
> the back. The other is a low building with only two square
> rooms and a fireplace in each, and a kitchen adjoining made
> of slab.

It was in this dwelling that McDonald, his wife, the former Jane Klyne and their young family were to live for the next four years.

> The outer work consists of three fields, each planted with
> thirty bushels of potatoes, and looks well. The provision shed,
> exclusive of table stores, is furnished with three thousand
> dried salmon, sixteen tierces salted ditto, thirty-six cwt. flour,
> two cwt. grease and thirty bushels salt.

And there were potatoes yet to be counted. Digging started late in October and was finished in the rain on November 15. So pleased was McDonald with the crop that he declared the occasion one for celebration—the first harvest festival. The yield, per bushel of seed, he proudly boasted, was twice that of the fertile lands of the Columbia Valley at Fort Vancouver. From 91 bushels of seed no less that 2,010 bushels had been gathered. So each man was given "a dram" and permission was granted for the holding of a dance. Fort Langley was prepared for the coming of winter.

From the day that he arrived McDonald was not allowed to forget that while the Clallam had been taught a lesson, the Yuculta held the white man in contempt. They said when they found it convenient, they would come and take the place. Just to keep the whites nervous, the Yuculta made frequent raids on the Musqueam and exacted tribute from other tribes. The *Whan-ee-tum* of Snugamish—the whitemen at Fort Langley—might be brave when faced by the Clallam. But the Yuculta! None could withstand their ferocity.

A meeting between the traders and the terrors of the coast was inevitable. It came on March 21, 1829. Yale, the courageous clerk who had fought against the Clallam, and Annance, the bold classical scholar, had been sent with ten men to take the accounts as far as the Cowlitz Portage. They were on their way home, had entered the Fraser River and were proceeding out of the channel between Annacis Island and the main shore when they saw, drawn up across the river barring their progress, nine great war canoes, each bearing between 25 and 30 howling, painted Yuculta braves.

Not for an instant did the paddling cease. Trained and trusted men made up that crew, the very best men from the fort, said McDonald in telling of the incident.

A whispered word between Yale and Annance, then a sharp order, and the paddles struck with greater vigor. Straight at the Yuculta line the boat leaped. The northeners, from whom men invariably fled, were taken completely by surprise. With a shout of defiance the Langley Express went through. Now the savages had to turn about. Bullets and arrows sprayed the water about the white men as they widened the gap between them and their enemies. None was hit. Now several of the canoes closer to shore sped ahead and landed warriors to harass the whites from the shore.

Suddenly the Langley crew swerved and made for the beach. Out sprang the two officers, followed by the men. They took cover and opened such a rapid fire that the Yuculta stopped trying to follow. How many were hit by the white men's bullets could not be ascertained. It was believed that casualties were high. The fight went on for a quarter of an hour. Then the raiders turned and paddled down river to the open sea as hard as they could go.

The *Whan-ee-tum* of Snugamish had met the Yuculta, not on even terms, but at twenty to one odds and had beaten them in fair fight! The news was almost incredible. The moccasin telegraph carried it from village to village. Indians gathered—from far and near to look upon men who could do such a thing.

McDonald was jubilant. It had demonstrated to the men themselves that the vandals from Johnstone Strait and Yuculta Rapids were no match for them. It had established that fact to native tribes who had existed in constant alarm of their oppressors.

"All the Indians hereabouts collected today and seem amazed at the victory gained over the invincible Yucultas, and that, too, by a handful of men," McDonald wrote in the journal.

Indian tradition says that having seen how the *Whan-ee-tum* were unafraid of the Yuculta, the Kwantlen decided to abandon their hereditary villages of Skaiametl and Kikait and cuddle beneath the wing of the fort. So they migrated up river and settled on Kanaka Creek directly opposite the fort, while a few established themselves on the same bank on the Fraser, close to the stockades. Here, they were convinced, they would be safe—and they were. The Yuculta came again only once. Then, as McMillan had predicted, "the iron interpreters" settled the argument.

It was in 1837, the storytellers say, that Yuculta came in great numbers. Each long canoe bore at least 20 warriors, and there were scores of canoes. Word of their approach was conveyed to the fort. The alarm was sounded. Men hastened to bastions and galleries. The cannons in the blockhouses were loaded with grape, swivel guns on the walls were packed with musket balls and small shot. The Kwantlen, and their allies the Musqueam and the Katzie, retreated before the invaders, and hid in the forest fringe.

Just before dusk the Yuculta fleet nosed around the Slikwhinna, and gathered for a dash at the village across the Stalo. With savage yells, intended to frighten their prey, the Yuculta armada shot diagonally across the river to within range of the death-crammed guns of the fort. Patiently the gunners awaited the word. It came at last, and from the bastions and galleries death and destruction poured upon the close-packed canoes.

The carnage was terrific. Canoes were blasted right out of the river; others splintered and sank; dead and dying mixed in the reddened, muddy waters. Then from the forests burst the Kwantlen with knives and spears. They and their allies started the work of butchery.

Few, if any, Yuculta escaped, tradition says. How many died in that final accounting when the Yuculta came to destroy the *Whan-ee-tum* of Snugamish, will never be known, but Kwantlen history maintains the total was several thousand. Suffice to say that the encounter broke the power of the Yuculta.

Archibald McDonald was not long installed as commander of Fort Langley when he made an inspection of the district, and expressed his surprise and disappointment that the post had been located at the site selected in 1827. The situation did not permit of cultivating the most desirable agricultural lands of the vicinity; the large prairie—Langley Prairie—on the T'salkwakyan Portage, over which the explorers of 1824 had come from the sea. Even the smaller area of arable land on the east side of the Salmon was too distant to be given ready protection from the fort. This, he found, had limited the possibilities of farming to the 15 acres already being utilized, of which only five acres comprised really good land.

McDonald was disappointed, but he did not let that fact retard his endeavors to make the best of what was available. He knew that it was good potato soil, but it did not show results he anticipated in grain crops. Then, too, part of the land was liable to flooding.

There was one crop, however, that delighted and amazed the canny Scot. It was the harvest of silver salmon that came up from the sea. Sufficient fish could be taken in a few weeks, while the runs were on, to feed year round every establishment west of the Rockies, he calculated. Here was the answer to Fort Langley's future. If these fish could be cured and shipped, a great export industry might be constructed. Out came paper and pencil, and McDonald computed that 7,544 salmon that had been traded from the Indians in 1829 had cost £13.17.10 in trade goods, or less than a ha'penny each! The average weight of the fish, he noted, was six pounds. Here, indeed, was potential profit. He decided to experiment with brine curing.

He wrote to the Governor and Committee in London about his dream of developing a fishery. He pointed out that already there was a store that might be utilized and a building in which coopers could be set to work. He was less enthusiastic about the agricultural possibilities of the place, observing:

> As to the farm, little can be said of it, all our operations that way being confined to the hoe. The elevated ground near the fort being already exhausted, did not yield us above 25 bushels wheat, 20 of pease and 10 of barley.

Governor Simpson, after his trip through the canyons of the Fraser, concluded that Fort Langley in its present location was not suitable for a main depot, "in the event of our being under the necessity of withdrawing from Fort Vancouver," even though it had served a useful purpose in obtaining a share of furs that otherwise would have gone to the Boston traders. In this work of driving the Americans from the coast, Fort Langley, in the first ten years of its existence, collected a total of 14,651 beaver skins, of which no less than 10,330 were large prime pelts. But in its earlier years the gathering of furs entailed a larger force than Simpson felt the returns warranted.

> The great population of this part of the country, and the hostile character they bear, renders it necessary to send a larger force among them than trade, in the first instance, could be expected to afford, as we are only respected by these treacherous savages in proportion to our strength and means of defence.

But that was written before the mighty Yuculta had been taught their lesson.

These reports reaching London created the impression that farming was both uncertain and unprofitable at Fort Langley. While McDonald was not optimistic as to the future of farming, he enthused about the fisheries, both salmon and sturgeon. In view of the fact that his vision was justified by the salmon trade becoming one of the world's great fisheries, McDonald's letter to Governor Simpson, under date of February 10, 1830, is of interest:

> In my last Communication I touched at some length on the prospect of curing Salmon at this place, as an additional source of Returns, and I have the satisfaction to inform you,

that the experiment of last Season completely proved the the-
ory; the fish, it is true, arrived late—indeed after we had
almost given up hopes of making anything at all of it; but from
the 20th of August to the 13th of the next month we were fortunate enough to procure upwards of 15,000; enough to make
up more than 200 Barrels, which in that very short space we
contrived to do, into nearly that number of casks of our own
making, with means so imperfect, however, that I fear from
the sample that remained with ourselves, the first Cargo will
not stand the Test of a foreign market, and trust by the next
Season, we shall be provided with a good Cooper, that will
know something of fish curing.

His fears were realized, for the barrels leaked, and the sample sent
to London did not win approval as an article for the market. But the
trade had possibilities, and eventually coopers were provided. There
was no hard wood for the manufacture of barrels, but a stand of white
pine was found on Work's River that flowed into the Fraser as some distance upstream, and which, by reason of the suitability of the wood,
became known as Stave River.

There was another objection to Fort Langley that carried weight
with those in authority, it was that shipping had to wait for a wind and
fair tide to make the trip up from the sea to the fort. This sometimes
caused loss of several days. The suggestion was advanced that Fort Langley should be removed to the coast. At first the head of Puget Sound,
where Fort Nisqually was later built, was favored. But while the plains
there were reported to be admirable for stock, they were not so adapt-
able to other forms of agricultural production. Then Whidby Island
came in for consideration and Francis Heron, chief trader, was instructed
to prepare to locate a post there.

But John McLoughlin, then at the height of his power and favor with
the Company, did not think it would be advisable to abandon the post
without making provision for the maintenance of the salmon fisheries.
In March, 1834, he wrote to Yale, who had by then succeeded to
McDonald's command of Fort Langley: "You will keep the fort in repair
and sow as much grain as you can."

Yale did not want to leave the Fraser. He too, envisioned the possibilities of the salmon fisheries. He believed as well that there were
opportunities to be developed in farming. He suggested that if it was
essential that Fort Langley be moved, then Lulu Island should be considered.

The exertions of Yale and McDonald had returned 2,062 large prime
beaver and 499 small ones—a record any post might boast about—for
the year 1833, and this had a bearing on the delay in final decision as to

abandonment. But in that same year, in London, the Committee came to a momentous decision. Steam vessels were now being used for deep sea voyages that were formerly considered impossible. In steam, it was thought, might be the answer to the problem of the Northwest Coast of America. Consequently a steamer was designed especially for the requirements of North Pacific waters.

The vessel was the *Beaver*. Of timbers of greenheart and oak was she built, with the latest in steam engines from the shops of Bolton and Watt. Launched in 1835, she reached the Columbia River the following year. The *Beaver* sailed from that place in the same year, to spend the next 53 years in the Inside Passage.

In the intervening years the sturdy craft had made history. Her contribution in retaining Fort Langley on the Fraser River was not the least of her services. Had the fort been moved, it is possible the flag she carried all her days might not have continued to fly north of the 49th parallel. In any event, the ease with which the steamer ran the distance from the mouth of the Fraser to Fort Langley removed one of the obstacles to the fort's continuance on the banks of the muddy river.

7

Fire and Religion

Fort Langley was crowded. It never was very commodious, even before McDonald had enlarged it to enclose a space 200 feet square. Now, however, with additional room required for cooperage and fish-curing it was becoming inconvenient. Besides it was poorly located in respect of the most arable lands in the vicinity.

James Murray Yale kept his little force of a dozen men busy. In addition to essential business, trafficking in furs with the Indians, or cultivating sufficient land to supply the establishment with some of its food requirements, the increasing demands of the export trade in cured salmon entailed much labor and attention. Salted fish was now being shipped regularly to Honolulu. Another phase of the fishery industry had developed in the manufacture of isinglass. This was made from the float bladder of the sturgeon, and as long as Yale remained in charge some hundreds of pounds were shipped each year, varying in price from six shillings a pound to as high as fourteen dollars during the Crimean war.

Yale had greater faith in the soil of the locality than had Archibald McDonald. Yale was anxious to try his hand at farming on a large scale, but that required a new and larger fort, situated in more arable land. Chief Factor Duncan Finlayson visited Fort Langley. Finlayson looked over the locality and selected what he thought would be a good site for a new establishment.

In 1838 McLoughlin was called to London to consult with the Governor and Committee of the Hudson's Bay Company, for great plans were in the making. Chief Trader James Douglas acted in his absence. Douglas was powerful of physique and possessed of a coldly analytical brain, and the ability to direct such men as Yale, whose worth he appreciated. Douglas envisioned good opportunities in farming as well as in fishing at Fort Langley. He wrote to Yale on November 21, 1838:

> I feel much gratified by the progressive improvement of the Farm and stock, in a few years Fort Langley will supply all the salt provisions required for the coast. The Salmon fishery is an object of much importance and merits the utmost attention.

> I am sorry that the site selected for the new Fort should be found subject to so many disadvantages, and we must therefore abandon it, and fix upon some other spot, alike convenient for the fur and Salmon trade, combined with facilities for the farm and shipping. Probably the place you first pointed out to Mr. Finlayson will be found on the whole most suitable, but if a better can be found, let it have preference; however remember that the Salmon trade must not be sacrificed, as it will always yield a more valuable return at less trouble, risk and expense than the farm.

This is what Yale wanted—a free hand. In Douglas he had a friend who would trust him. He went to work with rare good will. The new site lay higher up the Fraser by several miles.

Once more fort-builders' axes cut deeply into the forests for suitable timber; pickets were felled and rafted down the river from several points upstream. Canadians with broadaxes squared logs for new bastions. Sandwich Islanders toiled methodically in the sawpits finishing lumber. When stockades and blockhouses were in place, work commenced tearing down and moving the buildings from the old fort. In a remarkably short time Fort Langley was ready to be shifted. The move was completed on June 25, 1839.

Yale boasted, in a letter to Governor Simpson, January 15, 1840:

> The affairs of Fort Langley are in as favorable a condition as could be expected. Our removal from the old place was affected by the 25th June, without aid. We had cleared, fenced and cropped a sufficiency of new ground to amply repay us for what we had abandoned and that cost several years' labor. We did not commence moving any part of the old fort until we had our square here well surrounded with pickets and bastions and a store made to receive the goods.

And Douglas, reporting to London, 14 October 1839, wrote:

> We have abandoned the old Langley Establishment which was in a dilapidated State, as well as inconvenient in some respect for the business, and removed all the effects, into a new Fort built a few miles higher up on the Banks of Fraser's River, the stockades of which, four block houses, and nearly all the necessary buildings are now erected. It is fully as convenient for the fur and Salmon Trade, as the former site, and moreover it possesses the important and desirable advantage of being much nearer the farm.

Fur returns were on the decline from Fort Langley, Douglas told London. That was to be expected since the arrival of the *Beaver*, which was a veritable mobile trading post. Still Langley was not doing too badly, for Yale had traded 1,025 beaver skins during 1839, an increase of 398 over the previous year's total.

Yale had done a magnificent job. He was entitled to be proud of it. Prospects were bright that spring of 1840 for Fort Langley to accomplish great things. The force of men at the fort had been augmented by several men and a bustling, apple-cheeked little Scottish woman, Mrs. Finlay, wife of one of the recruits. She was an expert butter-maker and he was a dairyman. A creamery was located within the fort and the big barns for the cattle that grazed on the lush meadows of the little prairie were located close at hand. From the farm on the Big Prairie hay and grain were barged down the twisting, winding, sluggish Salmon to be stored in sheds erected near its confluence with the Fraser. Later these were replaced by larger buildings where the village of Fort Langley is now located.

Indians, impressed by the mastery of the *Whan-ee-tum* over the Yuculta, moved with the white men from Snugamish, and located on McMillan Island, where they built a new home, named for themselves, Kwantlen. They were copying the whites. Men who could defeat the warriors of Johnstone Strait and Yuculta Rapids, and yet would cheerfully do the work squaws alone should undertake—such men were puzzling, but worthy of imitation. Douglas was able to report to London:

> I may be permitted to mention...as a matter likely to interest the friends of our native population, and all who desire to trace the first dawn and early progress of civilization, that the Cowegians around Fort Langley, influenced by the counsel and example of the fort, are beginning to cultivate the soil, many of them having with great perseverance and industry cleared patches of forest land of sufficient extent to plant, each ten bushels of potatoes; the same spirit of enterprise extends, though less generally, to the Gulf of Georgia and de Fuca's straits, where the very novel sight of flourishing fields of pota-

toes satisfies the missionary visitors that the Honourable Company neither oppose, nor feel indifferent to, the march of improvement.

While Yale was building his new fort, Sir George Simpson was at Hamburg, Germany, discussing with Baron Ferdinand Wrangell, representing the Russian American Company something that would add to the importance of Fort Langley. It was a lease, by the Hudson's Bay Company, of part of what is now known as Southeastern Alaska, then part of Russian Alaska. Relations between the two great trading organizations had not been good. It was thought that by coming to an understanding with the Russians it would be easier to drive the American traders from the coast, because the Boston men received supplies from Russian posts.

Negotiations resulted in an agreement, signed on February 6, 1839. By its provisions the Hudson's Bay Company was to pay rental, for the territory involved, in land otter skins. It also agreed to sell certain agricultural products at fixed prices. The Company was obligated to provide 2,000 fenagos of wheat in 1839 and double that amount annually thereafter. A fenago was 126 pounds. Other supplies included 30 cwt. peas; 160 cwt. wheat flour; 130 cwt. grits and pot barley; 160 cwt. butter; 300 cwt. salted beef, and 30 cwt. of pork hams.

Fort Vancouver had extensive farms; Nisqually had fine possibilities for stock raising, and the Cowlitz lands could be developed, so with the incentive of the Russian agreement, great plans were made for farming. The Puget Sound Agricultural Association, a parallel company to the Hudson's Bay Company, was organized to direct the work. But the program of the new concern did not contemplate taking over Fort Langley's lush lands. Yale was capable of handling their development, and he did.

But McLoughlin, Douglas and others in authority urged the little man to great endeavors. They promised him every possible aid, and even sent him some laborers in addition to the Finlay family. One of these new arrivals was Jason Ovid Allard, the likeable, hard working, able nephew of a Point Levis notary. He became a very useful man, and as interpreter and postmaster won esteem among Indians and whites. He soon cemented affiliation between the Cowichan and the fort by marrying T'seeyiya, sister of the great Shashia. She adopted the name Justine.

Among the new arrivals was a Canadian named Brulé, from Fort Vancouver. A small hut was being constructed for him, and in the meantime he was permitted to occupy part of the blacksmith shop. Just what happened is uncertain, but on the night of 11 April 1840, while Brulé was absent from his quarters, flames broke out from the smithy. Instantly the cry of "Fire!" rang out and the alarm was sounded. Before the men of the fort could assemble, however, other buildings and the stockade itself were ablaze.

"Quick," shouted Yale, "the powder!" Barrels of black powder were trundled from the bastions and the magazine to a place of safety. Then the men tried to save the trade goods. From already burning buildings they carried bundles of blankets and other merchandise, so necessary for them to have if they were to secure the cooperation of the Indians.

Mrs. Finlay was perhaps the most excited person there. She ran about shouting excitedly for some one to save the cream that she had set out in pans. At last she attracted attention and several men helped her to carry the big shallow pans beyond the flaming stockade. A moment later someone upset them. In her excitement the good wife had forgotten her baby. Just in time Allard dashed into the burning building to bring it to safety.

As the burning fort illuminated the skies, canoes by the dozen came from Kwantlen, from Kanaka Creek and from even below Slikwhinna. Indians crowded about the fire, getting in the way of the whites, seeking a chance to pick up loot.

When morning came only hot ashes and charred and blackened stumps remained of the fort of which Yale had been so proud. The commander could take stock of the extent of disaster. A few furs had been saved, the bulk of the trading goods, eleven muskets and the powder, seven barrels of salmon and three or four "old implements for building." The rest of the stock, barrels for pickling salmon and all the rest was gone.

But Yale had no time to repine. Fortunately several rafts of pickets, intended for the farms, were available. The men commenced at once to putting up a temporary stockade. In an incredibly short time a defensive work of 70 by 108 feet was erected. As soon as this was finished, the indefatigable Yale commenced construction of a new and bigger fort.

Chief Trader Douglas was on his way to Puget Sound to board the *Beaver* for Alaska when, at Cowlitz Portage, he learned of the destruction of Fort Langley. He hastened to the Sound and ordered the steamer to make all speed to the Fraser. He arrived on 1 May where he found Yale secure. Peppery "Little Yale" bluntly told the gigantic Douglas, "All I want from you is that you give me six axes and be off." But Douglas stayed several days, put 20 men to help finish a bastion and in cutting and squaring logs for a building. This done, he was convinced the temporary fort was secure. "The work of destruction has been fearfully complete," he noted in his journal, "extending to every part of the premises, of which a few blackened stumps alone remain." And then Douglas went his way.

With such purpose did Yale labor at rebuilding, that by 10 February 1841 (ten months after the destruction of the post) he was able to write Governor George Simpson:

> The whole total affairs of Fort Langley would hardly seem to have met with a check. Nearly everything that could be done in the way of Farming was accomplished. The Salmon fishery in due time reestablished—that is in the necessary buildings. Vessels for pickling the fish in, etc.—and in regard to the business of the Dairy, it would appear that we may carry the feather.

> Have a Fort far more spacious than the old one, and things inside nearly as far advanced towards a completion as Fort Langley was when you first visited it, the second year after it was established.

It was, indeed, a spacious fort, constructed on a ridge overlooking the verdant fields of the lowlands. It was enlarged slightly some years later, when it had a length of 630 feet by a width of 240 feet—one of the largest forts built by the Hudson's Bay Company. Yale also told Simpson that:

> Last winter Chief Factor McLoughlin proposed to send us plenty of aid to get in the crops, etc., but unluckily the [unintelligible] had apparently become great, none could be spared, he has however tho' rather late consoled me a little by sending Fort Langley an old broken threshing Mill.

Yale was irritated because McLoughlin had taken some of his cattle from him. Douglas tells of what happened. On the latter's return from Alaska in September he called at Fort Langley, where he found instructions from McLoughlin to remove as many cattle as the *Beaver* could carry. Yale was angry. He stormed that he could provide food for three times as many animals. "However," Douglas wrote, "his wishes were not to be consulted." Douglas well knew McLoughlin's hasty temper. He had ordered the beasts to be shifted, and shifted some at least must be. Douglas sympathized with his friend and he compromised by taking only 11 head although the steamer could carry 25.

The observant Douglas noted that the outlook for farming operations was for a harvest of 500 bushels of fall wheat and 250 bushels spring wheat; 300 bushels of barley; 600 of peas and 500 of oats. The potato harvest promised to be abundant.

It was a fine fort, was this last Fort Langley. Within its walls were all necessary buildings, spaced well apart to isolate fire, a provision that twice saved the establishment from complete destruction. It was a pleasant spot, where the personnel fared better than at any other post, except Fort Vancouver, the great emporium of the Hudson's Bay Company's west. Yale could well congratulate himself on the harmony that had been established since the defeat of the Yuculta. Peace reigned—as far, at least, as the white men on the Stalo were concerned.

Fort Langley, however, was to have a new experience. Religion was at hand. It was coming to the Halkomelem, and even to their ancient enemies. The 'Cross was raised' on the banks of the Fraser in the summer of 1841. Father Modeste Demers had crossed the continent with Father Francis Norbert Blanchet, newly-appointed vicar-general under the Monsignor of Juliopolis, Quebec, to minister to the Indians and whites of the Pacific Slope. Great men were these pioneer Catholic missioners, who attained to high honors in the Church and won the esteem of men of all creeds by their principles of service and self sacrifice.

Father Blanchet had visited Puget Sound and had instructed the Indians in 1840, and now—the next year—Father Demers was extending the mission to the Fraser River. Describing the trip to officials in Quebec, he wrote:

> I arrived toward evening at the entrance of an inlet or vast bay, called Biret Bay, where my guides told me we would have to make a difficult portage before reaching the prairie upon which Fort Langley farm is found. Indeed, the following day we travelled for ten hours, and arrived exhausted and fatigued at the entrance of a prairie, where I met a Canadian who was awaiting me with a horse. The farm is three miles from the Fort.

> Mr. Yale, commandant of the fort, sent men with horses to transfer our baggage, and I finally arrived at the post, where I was received with hoisted flag and a salute of seven cannons. This was a brilliant occasion. The welcome that Mr. Yale extended me was such as would be expected by a man of merit and distinction. Five or six hundred savages instantly surrounded me and I had difficulty getting out of their midst to enter the fort.

> Destroyed in 1840 by fire, this post has since been rebuilt on a larger, more beautiful plan. A score of men are employed as agricultural laborers. Eight of whom are Canadians, one Iroquois and the others Kanakas, natives of the Sandwich Islands; all have wives and children in the manner of the country. I baptised fifteen children, including those of Mr. Yale, and gave instructions to others, older, who did not even know the Lord's Prayer.

A two-views-in-one sketch of Fort Langley. In the foreground is a close-up view of the area directly below the northeast bastion. In the background the fort and wharf are seen from the opposite bank of the river.

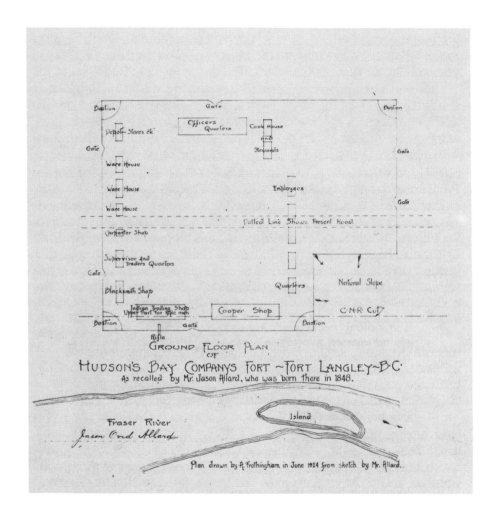

GROUND FLOOR PLAN
OF
HUDSON'S BAY COMPANYS FORT ~FORT LANGLEY~B·C·
As recalled by Mr. Jason Allard, who was born there in 1848.

Fraser River

Jason Ovid Allard.

Island

Plan drawn by A. Frothingham in June 1924 from sketch by Mr. Allard.

In 1924, A. Frothingham drew this plan of Fort Langley. He based it on a sketch draw from memory by Jason Allard, who was born at the fort in 1848.

In this 1858 sketch by E. Mallandaine, the Big House stands at the right; to the left there is the southeast bastion, a depot, and warehouse. The alleyway between the depot and warehouse led to a gate in the palisades.

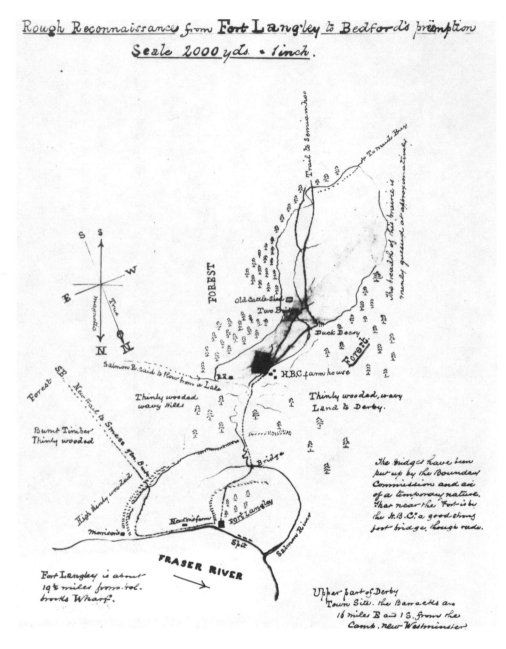

Fort Langley and environs probably about 1860 as settlement had begun. Trails at the top of the map led to present-day White Rock area.

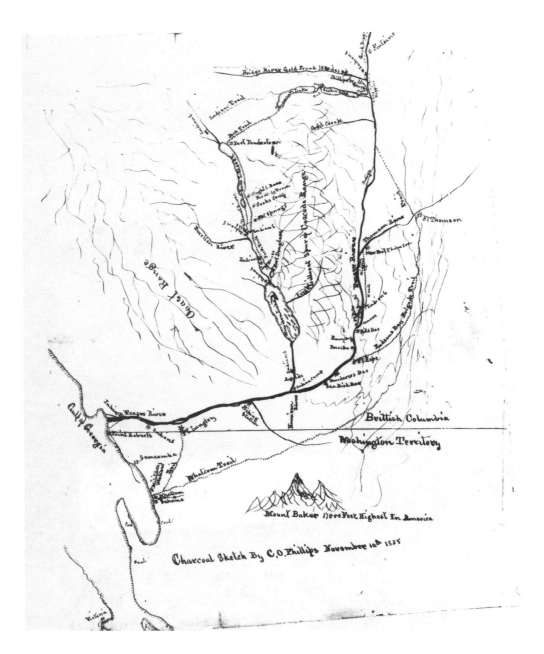

Sketch of gold-rush area, Victoria to Bridge River. Note the Whatcom Trail, one of the best-known shortcuts to the gold fields in 1858.

Palisades and cooperage at the time of the British Columbia Centennial, 1958.

Cooperage with finished barrels ready to be moved to the fish processing sheds.

The Big House, or Officer's Quarters; to the right a white-wall tent, freshly-sawn timbers, and cart used for construction and freighting.

Father Demers' mission was primarily to the Indians. He turned his attention to instructing them and so came into contact with the Yuculta. He had heard of them as soon as he reached Puget Sound. Now he was to meet them, especially one of their great war leaders. The fact that this chief was at Fort Langley testified that an alliance existed between the Yuculta and the Stalo people. Such a peace could only have been sued for by the Northerners; Yale could not have so risked the white man's prestige. In his report home, the priest continued:

> I had the pleasure of making the acquaintance of a chief of the Yougletas, who by a recent alliance was found among the different nations whom I instructed. This man of remarkable stature and outstanding because of his stately bearing, had a forehead high and wide, and hair long and thrown back. He was constantly at all the instructions and even had one of his children baptised. 'I am wicked,' he told me one day. He spoke very truly when he declared himself wicked, for savages here assured me that in warring with other nations, to cut off a head and take it to his mouth to drink the blood flowing from it is an action wholly to his taste.

Yet, this bloodthirsty chief was so impressed he offered to carry the message of Christianity to his people.

In describing the phenomenal success of the mission, Father Demers told of how he baptised a total of more than four hundred. "The assemblies were held a short distance from the Fort gate in a low, level prairie," he explained. "I was continually surrounded by fifteen to sixteen hundred adult savages, understanding my instructions, all listening attentively and with an incredible order."

For several days the teachings went on, and each day was featured by baptisms, until his arms ached, he said. "All these nations had forgotten their hates and plans for vengeance in order to come and listen to the Word of God in common. Several injuries had not been atoned and vengeance was only being suspended. That is why they at first came to the instructions suspiciously, and arrived with guns that I soon had disposed at my feet...It was an extraordinary feat and the result of visible protection from Heaven that in reassembling so many different nations by their interests, language and customs no quarrel was brought up."

Now, from away up the river, came word that a tribe was anxious to meet the black-gowned medicine man, but that they feared their ancient enemies. Word was sent to them to come and they would be received in peace. The next day 306 of them arrived. "Everyone placed himself in line in order to give the indispensable greeting," remarked the priest, "and I had to extend my hand to three hundred and six persons, while I held the other raised above my head."

Now, after more than a week, Father Demers had to leave Fort Langley to return to the Columbia. So, on September 8 in closing his mission he distributed all his remaining religious medals and a stock of tobacco—for the Indians had become addicted to the weed since those days when Simon Fraser astonished them by inhaling smoke.

"There was great smoking," the priest wrote home.

8

New Fur Trails

James Murray Yale was happy in his new fort. It was beautifully and conveniently situated, but he soon found that expanded activities he had undertaken were difficult of accomplishment with the force at his command. He had gone ahead with such vigor in bringing land under cultivation that he soon had 240 acres broken, while 195 neat cattle and 180 pigs required somebody's constant attention. He had but 20 men at his command. They must, in addition to agricultural pursuits, cut timber at Stave River and float it down to the fort for the manufacture of barrels, tubs and kegs for the salmon fishery.

Then too, there were the demands of the fur trade to be met, and, as always, the ceaseless guarding of the establishment. There were 15 horses at the post, but the men worked harder than did the beasts. But they fared well. While Yale was a hard-driving master he was just, and so they worked willingly.

McDonald and Yale had started an industry that was to grow into a world-export trade when they began curing Fraser River salmon. McLoughlin saw in it some immediate profit to compensate for the decline in fur returns from Fort Langley. Douglas envisioned the day when the fisheries would replace the combined values of furs and farms.

Mrs. Aurelia Manson, daughter of Chief Trader Yale—for he had, in 1844, received deserved although belated promotion—left an interesting glimpse of the commencement of British Columbia salmon fisheries, as she remembered it:

> Ovid Allard was postmaster; that is he had charge of the Indians and the keys of the fort. Many a time have I heard him calling out the time for the people to go out, and of course all strangers would hurry out.
>
> I used to visit him when he was trading with the Indians for their cranberries, hazelnuts and fish.
>
> The blacksmith's shop was a wonderful place for me. The smith made nails of different sizes, and iron hoops for the kegs, barrels and vats that were being made by the cooper, W. Cromarty, with his three or four assistants, getting ready for the salmon run.
>
> Ovid Allard did all the trading with the natives for their salmon. He used to stand at the wharf with two or three trunks full of the Indians' favorite stuffs, such as vermillion for the women to give themselves rosy cheeks, and tobacco for the men.
>
> Cromarty would be at the big cauldron making brine, and ever so many boys, and a man or two, would be running from the wharf with salmon, which they piled before the women of the fort and others who were seated in a circle in the shed where they cut the salmon. No rest for the boys! They had to continue their running; this time with the cut salmon to the men in the big shed where they were doing the salting. So they worked all the week; early in the morning until late at night, until the salmon run was over.

Yale, himself, could measure the potentialities of the place better than could officials who seldom, if ever, visited Fort Langley. His views, about the second year after the fire, were contained in a letter to Sir George Simpson—for a grateful sovereign had rewarded the Governor for his services to Crown and Empire:

> The Salmon trade, so far as regards quantity is likely to continue productive. Our farm is well established with buildings and fences and quite extensive enough, having now more cultivated ground than we are able to till in the course of a season, exclusive of a reserve for winter wheat; but the climate is unfavorable and the soil ill adapted to its disadvantages, being low and wet, and making the suitable time for ploughing, sowing and harvest exceedingly backward and we have been and still continue to be ill provided with means to obviate these local obstacles. The part of the Establishment consti-

tuting the Fort with the outdoor building for curing Salmon in
&c. affords every desirable convenience.

While the trade in salmon made up the major part of the fishery out-
put of Fort Langley, it did not include all the wealth of the river that Yale
garnered for the Company. He manufactured from 300 to 800 pounds
annually of isinglass. This rare product was valued for inventory pur-
poses at six shillings a pound, although during the Crimean war San
Francisco bid as high as $14 a pound for this product of the Fraser. Eula-
chon were also cured to some extent, while Yale also tried his hand at
making caviar. The recipe for making this delicacy was obtained from
Russia as part of the deal for the lease on Alaskan territory.

And while the ink was still drying on Yale's commission as chief
trader, great events, affecting the future of Fort Langley, were shaping at
London and Washington. The results of Captain Black's folly when he
smashed the bottle of wine on the flagstaff at Astoria were being realized. United States was laying claim anew to the whole of the western
slope, north of latitude 42 to the Russian line at 54 degrees 40 minutes.
British statesmen were confident that they would be able to hold the
boundary at latitude 49.

Such a demarkation had been suggested as early as 1818. But in
those early times little was known of the country and the location of the
mouth of the Fraser River had not been precisely determined. Now,
however, in the early years of "the fateful forties" the great worth of the
Fraser with its silver treasure in fish was realized. The Strait of Juan de
Fuca must be kept open as a corridor to the second great river of the
west, for if the 49th parallel was followed to the ocean it would bisect
Vancouver Island, and British shipping might be forced to thread the
dangerous waters of Johnstone Strait to reach Fort Langley. The establishment of the post on the Fraser had helped to hold the country for
Great Britain, for it was established British occupancy. In 1843, under
orders from the Governor and Committee in London, on suggestion of
Sir George Simpson, the southern tip of Vancouver Island was occupied,
and Fort Victoria, named after the young and popular sovereign was
constructed.

In 1829 Simpson had explained:

> Fort Langley was established with the double object of secur-
> ing a share of the Coasting trade which had previously been
> monopolised by the Americans, and of possessing a settle-
> ment on the Coast which would answer the purpose of a
> Depot, in the event of our being under the necessity of with-
> drawing from Fort Vancouver.

Fort Victoria, it was determined, might be used as a main depot in the future, but Fort Langley would form an admirable brigade terminus and supply base. So it was regarded when, in the summer of 1846, the boundary was established, leaving the whole of Vancouver Island to Great Britain. British traders were supposed, under the treaty, to have equal rights with Americans in the navigation of the Columbia River, but it was soon found that United States customs officers did not place such an interpretation upon the treaty. The construction of a new route into the Thompson River and New Caledonia districts must be undertaken.

In charge at Fort Alexandria, the gateway to the Chilcotin Plateau, was Alexander Caulfield Anderson, an enterprising and well educated clerk. Anderson, who was destined to play many important roles in the development of the Pacific Coast, was born in India, the son of a former British army officer who had taken up indigo planting. The boy, with his brother, had been sent to England to be educated; later they entered the fur trade as apprentices. A. C. Anderson was a born explorer and geographer, and a keen naturalist, an ability that he had inherited from his famous grandsire Dr. James Anderson, the noted Scottish botanist who was a correspondent of George Washington.

Anderson followed with keen interest the slow moving news of the negotiations between the two powers that seeped through to his lonely establishment. Someone should be looking for a new route while the diplomats argued, he reasoned; so he wrote to Sir George Simpson offering to explore for a way to Fort Langley from Fort Kamloops at the forks of the Thompson River. His offer was gladly accepted, James Douglas and Peter Skene Ogden welcoming the news that the Governor and Council had accepted Anderson's offer. Chief Factor Ogden, remembering that Archibald McDonald venturing west of the Fraser from Pavillon Lake had reached the Lillooet River flowing into Harrison Lake and into the Fraser not very far from Fort Langley, suggested that Anderson first explore this possibility.

It was on May 15, 1846 that Anderson with a party of five left Kamloops. He passed down Kamloops Lake and along the Thompson and up the Bonaparte to Hat Creek, and on through Marble Canyon, the beauties of which deeply impressed him. At last they came to the Fraser River at the mouth of present Cayoosh Creek and went up that stream and Seton River to beautiful Seton Lake—which bears the name of Colonel Alexander Seton, a near relative of Anderson's. The bold, rocky ramparts of that lake did not indicate ease of construction of a brigade trail— but the lake could be travelled by batteaux.

So down the lake went the explorers, and across the narrow neck of land that separated Seton from another attractive large lake—which later obtained the name of Anderson himself—and so by way of Gates, Birkenhead and Lillooet rivers to Harrison Lake, and on to Fort Langley, where he arrived on May 24. The way was not difficult, but it would require frequent use of batteaux.

After a four-day rest, Anderson and his party started on a more difficult journey. They had heard of Indians crossing from the Okanagan and Similkameen countries to the Fraser. They started to find how they came. He went up the river to Silver Creek, but the trail that might be made that way would not be practical for horses; so he returned and entered the mountains again by way of the Coquihalla River valley, which he followed until he came to the Nicolum Creek, and then by a stream he called the Simil-a-ouch—but which is now known as the Sumallo—to Skagit River. He followed the Skagit to Snass River. He proceeded up the east fork of the Snass to its headwaters and crossed the divide to the Tulameen.

He met, by appointment, an Indian named Blackeye, whom he had ordered to meet him there before he had left Kamloops. He had intended to cross to the Red Earth Forks, near the site of the present Princeton, but Blackeye advised a shortcut by way of Otter, Myran and Guilford creeks to Quilchena Creek and Nicola Lake. This was accomplished without difficulty, and the usual road from Nicola Lake to Kamloops was followed.

The following year Anderson went out again. The boundary line had been fixed, and the need of a new route to the sea was urgent. The Board of Management—for Dr. McLoughlin had retired—felt that the Coquihalla route might delay brigades unduly by reason of snow lingering well on into the summer on the higher levels. Therefore Anderson was advised to try and break through the Fraser Canyon.

He found that it was impractical to build a horse trail down the Thompson to the forks—where Lytton stands today—and from that point through the difficult country along the Fraser, so he went to Nicola Lake and made a hazardous and exhausting trip through the mountains, coming out at Kequeloose, an Indian village on the river. He managed to cross to the other side and found that it was possible, but dangerous, to transport goods through the mountain barrier by making use of batteaux and portaging at several especially difficult bits of water. The route from Nicola Lake to Kequeloose had been by way of Nicola River to Coldwater River, up that stream for 20 miles, where Spius Creek, a branch of Uztlius Creek, a tributary of Anderson River was crossed. From the Anderson the way led to the Fraser.

Douglas, however, was not satisfied with the proposal to risk the passage from Kequeloose to "The Falls"—where Fort Yale was later established—by the water route. So he and Chief Factor John Work, who had succeeded to the Board of Management on the retirement of Ogden, came to Fort Langley.

What a change! Work found the muddy prairies where he had commented upon the growth of rich grass for wandering bands of elk, now smiling fields of grain, while domestic cattle grazed contentedly within sight on one of the largest posts that the Hudson's Bay Company possessed. Old Whattlekainum was not there to greet him, but the aging Shashia gave him welcome.

Douglas took Yale and William Sinclair with him to investigate the Canyon route. John Work was left in charge of the establishment that had eventuated from that trip when, twenty-three years before, he and James McMillan, Thomas McKay, Annance, Laframboise, with the voluable Jean Ba'tiste Proveau and others had crossed the T'salkwakyan Portage from the sea.

Douglas and Yale found an Indian track that left the river and passed by way of a mountain defile to come down a slope to meet the river again at Spuzzum. Douglas was delighted. He was sure that a feasible road could be constructed. Yale was not so optimistic, so he indelibly associated his superior with its selection by naming it the Douglas Portage. It was realized that a great deal of work would have to be done, not only on this portage, but on the whole route to make it into anything like a good brigade trail. It was hoped that it might be got ready by 1849.

Then, late in 1847, came the murders of Dr. Marcus Whitman, his wife and members of his mission, at Waiilatpu, in the Oregon Territory, and the consequent unrest amongst the Indian tribes, who were unhappy about the new rule of their country. This made it dangerous for the brigades to follow the old route to the Columbia. This risk was too great to permit waiting for the improvement of the trail.

So orders were given that Donald Manson, in charge of the New Caledonia brigade, with his furs and those gathered by John Tod at Kamloops, must force their way, via Anderson's Kequeloose route to Fort Langley during the summer of 1848. Anderson was to lead the way. It was a terrible journey, exhausting both men and horses. Beasts toppled down hillsides, and only the most arduous efforts on the part of the men, and the courage of their leaders brought the brigade through.

In the meanwhile Yale had sent Ovid Allard to construct a store and stopping place at the foot of the falls—which he named in honor of the Fort Langley commander—and another, just a big house, at Spuzzum where the brigade was ferried across the river. This was named Simon's

House. Batteaux were built there and more were constructed at Fort Langley and sent up the river. At last the brigade reached Fort Yale, and the horses were left there, while the goods and men were transferred to the boats to drift down to the good fare and fun of that well-found establishment.

When, on July 17, Manson started to return, he found that five of his men had deserted rather than face the terrors of a second trip over the trail. He had trouble with them all the while they were at Fort Langley when the preparations for the return journey were being made. Now, however, he got them, grumbling mightily, into the batteaux and the start was made. It took eight days to make the distance between Fort Langley and Fort Yale. There further delays were required to round up the horses and arrange the packs. There was very little horse feed at Fort Yale, and the big band of horses soon had all the grass in the vicinity eaten. The result was that they were weak and hungry when they were called upon to start freighting through the mountains again.

Henry Newsham Peers, a clerk in the Company's service, went with the brigade, and he kept a diary. It is typical of the toil and dangerous travel of the fur trails. He tells how, in order to ease the horses, "half the goods...were carried over the river portage by 80 Indians in three or four trips." This was along the Indian trail that clung precariously to the canyons. Thirty-five horses, the best of them, were used to take the balance of the merchandise by way of Douglas Portage, making three or four trips. Two horses rolled down the mountain slopes. It was a difficult and exacting trip—a foretaste of days to come.

The brigade required three days to rest the men and horses and rearrange the merchandise at Spuzzum, and to ferry the horses across the river. It was August 6 when a start was made again,

> with some five hundred and upwards pieces of goods in 15
> brigades, each brigade having 18 and some a greater number
> of horses and two men. We encamped at the foot of the Big
> Hill where the road leaves Fraser River, many of the brigades
> only arriving when pitch dark and consequently great confu-
> sion from horses straying with their loads and so forth; several
> fell down a steep hill on nearing the encampment...from
> weakness, threw their loads and a bale was swept off in the
> river...and one animal killed.

It had been a terrible day. One poor fellow was so tortured in mind and body that he crawled away during the night and committed suicide, rather than endure the rest of the trip. He was buried on the spot. Father John Nobili, who accompanied the men, conducting a brief ceremony before the brigades moved on.

Day after day the brigades, with Anderson doggedly leading the way fought their way onward, the weakened horses unable to find grass in that rugged country, falling and stumbling from sheer exhaustion. One night 80 pieces of freight were missing when the stop was made at the close of daylight. A halt had to be made the next day while search was made for the goods. Indians were enlisted for the purpose. On 12 August Peers recorded:

> It was our intention to have reached the height of land today, but from the jaded state of our animals and the general confusion among the rear brigades we were obliged to camp in the woods...Here again was a sad account of the goods, many pieces left on the road and three parties obliged to halt, separated one from another, night having overtaken them before they could reach the camp.

Such an entry was typical of that journey.

Finally, when the height of land was passed and they had progressed a little way towards the Nicola country, they found fresh horses waiting. The balance of the way presented no trouble, and at last they reached Fort Kamloops to count the cost; some 70 horses had been lost, of which 27 had died on the return trip; much property had been destroyed or was missing, and one man had died.

It was clear that this route was not satisfactory in its present state, nor could it be improved without much expense and toil. It was a gloomy council of war that Manson, Tod and Anderson held at Fort Kamloops. What was to be done? The answer Anderson was certain, was to try the route that he favored most, via the Coquihalla. So the three gave written instructions to Peers to try and lay out a road through by that way. And Peers did so in 1847.

He found that by varying slightly Anderson's track he could avoid one or two difficult places. The work of opening the trail went forward, and it became the main route for the argosies of the North to reach the sea until after the construction of the Cariboo Road.

Fort Yale was now temporarily abandoned, and Peers was sent to build a new post near the mouth of the Coquihalla. Here, on a nice, grass-covered flat, admirably suited for a horse depot, he built Fort Hope.

And at Fort Langley, Yale was having his troubles. The winter of 1847-48 was the most severe that the memory of the oldest Indian could recall. Many cattle died, and others were taken into the Indians' huts for shelter. The making of Fort Langley the terminus of the brigades placed new responsibilities and more work on the shoulders of Yale. The demands in the export markets for Fraser River salmon were increasing.

Yale decided to locate a fishery at the mouth of Harrison River. He could not afford to place a white man in charge, so he hired an Indian. In July, just when he was looking for good returns from this venture, the station was burned to the ground.

But this was not the only loss by fire. "On the 26th November," he reported to Governor Simpson, "we experienced a great disaster. One of our sheds, the most spacious and staple built of the sort (with the adjoining shed for threshing in) and its contents, about 800 bus. Oats. The whole crop of Peas and Barley and a quantity of fodder, reserve of the year before, was totally destroyed."

Some boys were hunting chicken nests in the shed, and, it being cold, started a fire for warmth. In a few minutes there was a flaming furnace, and the adjoining structure was aflame. Now the wisdom of Yale having built a large fort was apparent, for the space between buildings gave the men a chance to fight the fire. The lesson of the second fort's construction had been well learned. But the loss was heavy. As a result of the loss of provender, more than 100 animals died.

Fire was always a menace, and once again Yale had to battle it, when in 1852 flames again threatened the place, but were confined to a single building.

But Fort Langley had come of age. It had reached manhood, and was fully established; it had come a long way from the little fort that McMillan had built and the Indians had called Snugamish, to have a definite place in the general economy of the Northwest Coast, with fisheries that were to become world famous, fair farms and an important position on the fur trails of the west.

9
Gold and Grief

The tremendous growth of the export trade in salmon, amounting to 2,000 barrels annually, and requiring manufacture of at least that number of large containers, and in addition kegs and casks for smaller fish and for cranberries, provided sufficient tasks for practically the whole force stationed at the fort. Then there were the extensive farms to be worked, the herds to be attended, the barter of the fur trade to be maintained and the fort to be kept up.

The cranberry trade was a new development; one that followed the growth of a large demand at San Francisco with the discovery of gold in California. Two free traders started it, Captain James Cooper, a settler on Vancouver Island, and a Captain Webster, of the *Honolulu Packet*. They induced the Indians to gather the berries that grew in profusion on the marshy lands of the Fraser delta.

It was in 1852 that Cooper arrived at Fort Langley. He wanted to buy barrels for the berries. Sufficient containers for his immediate wants were sold to him by Allard. Later when Douglas rapped the knuckles of Yale for encouraging trade by unauthorized individuals on the river, Yale upbraided Allard, who in turn asserted that Yale had sanctioned the sale. The result of the quarrel was that Allard quit Fort Langley. He was transferred to Nanaimo, where coal had been discovered, and became superintendent of Indian labor there. He was a great loss to Yale; Allard had been his right-hand man.

Conditions had changed of late years, and each alteration of the old system seemed to irk Yale. In 1849 the Board of Management moved from the Columbia River to Fort Victoria, which became the headquarters for the Company's affairs on the Pacific Slope. Douglas was the first to transfer his abode to the Island. John Work, his coadjutor and the assenting member of the Board, was sent to the northern coast to personally supervise operations there, while Douglas carried on the principal direction of the business. He was soon wielding even greater power than had Dr. McLoughlin, and with more efficiency and greater tact.

The same year that the fort on Camosun Harbour became the official seat of the Company's operations west of the Rockies, the British government had created Vancouver Island a Crown Colony in 1849, and having thus asserted the right and dominion of the Crown, it was leased to the Company for ten years. Conditional upon this lease was a guarantee to encourage settlement. Richard Blanshard was sent out as governor. He stayed less than a year, retiring in 1851 to be succeeded by James Douglas.

Yale did not like these changes, and particularly the selection of Fort Victoria as headquarters. He would have preferred being at a greater distance from the Board of Management. He was too convenient. "Let Yale do it," appeared to become an easy way to shift burdens. The coal mines at Fort Rupert had proved to be failure; new deposits were required—Yale could find them. He did. He discovered thin seams away up Kanaka Creek, opposite the original fort, and "between the North channel of Fraser's River and Burrard Canal." Fortunately, however, for his peace of mind splendid outcroppings were revealed by an Indian at Wenthuysen Inlet where Nanaimo was then built.

Foodstuffs were required for the Interior posts; the supplies of grain and flour had formerly come from the broad acres at Fort Vancouver—Yale could make up the deficiency. He was instructed to put more and more land under tillage, and was promised six good farm hands. He received four men and had to send three of them back to Fort Victoria as being useless. And so Yale and his meagre force worked and strained to meet each new demand made upon them.

The annual brigades arriving and staying—sometimes for weeks—disrupted the whole smooth economy of the place. Jason Ovid Allard II, the son of Yale's assistant, has left a description of the arrival of the brigades. He tells of how firing would be heard from up the river. Then the batteaux laden with the baled furs of the north would stop at the island off Whonnock, where the men would don their best clothes and decorate themselves with gay ribbons. Then they would push off, singing old

Canadian boat songs, punctuating the melody by the firing of small arms.

Now the cannon from the bastions would blast out a welcome and the populace of the place would hasten out of the gates to the riverside to cheer and wave greetings to the oncoming boats. All would be excitement. The freight would be quickly unloaded and be carried to safety in the warehouses. This done, half a gill of rum would be dished out to each man—the regale was on! More strong liquor could be purchased. For several days and nights there would be dancing and feasting, and drinking and fighting; a happy time would be the measure of everyone. It was a merry break in the monotony, but it played havoc with the efforts of Yale to produce foodstuffs to a maximum.

Such things slowed up operations. Yale did not like the delay and the confusion caused by the brigades. Nor did he care to have Chief Factor Douglas too often about the place. It was not that he did not like the great man, for he did, and Douglas held Yale in high esteem, but the towering and somewhat pompous governor had a secret delight. It was to stand beside wee Yale and look down upon him from his six feet two inches. It amused him to see how Yale would quickly move to avoid the inevitable comparison between their stature. It was not this, however, that bothered Fort Langley's commander. It was that those who did not understand conditions blamed him for the decline in fur returns from the upper Stalo country. One of the reasons for this falling off in skins was that it was too easy for Indians to cross the Strait of Georgia to Fort Victoria.

He became quite vexed over the whole thing, and poured out his heart to his old friend of Athabasca days before Union, Sir George Simpson, in a letter dated in October 1852. There was, he asserted: "a seeming necessity of superior powers" to bring the functions of the "highly respected but rather singular body the Board of Management, to bear upon a concentrated course, and restore the Company's affairs in these quarters to a more wholesome condition." He was not going to stand for being blamed for conditions that he could not control, nor was he going to have the good name of Fort Langley sullied by unwarranted criticism. He strained his vocabulary in vigorous refutation of baseless innuendoes.

> The greatest evils here seem to spring out of Vancouver's Island," he declared. "It would be ungenerous and to cause no salutary consequences, to cast reflections derogatory to the business of Fort Langley. [sic] It has resisted many tendencies to obstruct its due course, and tho' much depreciated, Old Langley stands still stable, the main prop of the Company's commerce on the North West Coast of America, and can not,

> with any show of reason, be reproached for anything, except, perhaps, that of affording maintenance to a rising Sodom on Vancouver's Island.
>
> A great part of the fur procured by the natives in the Interior within the Langley precincts are taken to Fort Victoria. The Indian traders here are glad to get a few furs to secure an ostentatious reception at the great emporium...and after seeing the World, and tasting of its sweets into the bargain, they come home loaded with goods. Then follow a host of laborers, all in the costumes of princes, and with wealth such as a few years ago would have been considered sufficient to maintain them in grandeur for an age.

No, Yale did not like the changed conditions. He wanted to have Fort Langley remain as it was when his old friends, Whattlekainum and Shashia were men of might on the Stalo. But they had passed out of the picture, and younger men ruled in their stead. Gone, too, was Tzouhalem the Wicked, the bluebeard of the Cowichan who emerged from his fort at Cowichan Bay, where he kept his many wives, to plunder and kill.

Yale did not mourn his violent death as he regretted the passing of the others. No, Tzouhalem had tried to murder him, and might have done so but for Allard. The Cowichan had hidden himself outside of the fort waiting for Yale to come out. The postmaster had learned of the ambush, and crept up from behind and pounced upon the Indian. He wrested his gun away from him and then booted him down the bank and into his canoe. Tzouhalem did not return.

The younger generation were not like their fathers. Yale could understand Indians in those days. Now the swaggering youths aped the ways and cultivated the vices of the whites. But all the protesting that he could do would not alter conditions, he had to conclude—but he did deplore them.

Now it was 1856, and the weary, discontented Yale and the powerful Douglas were to encounter new worries and difficulties as the result of the happenings of that year. Perhaps, if old Tent-a-coose—who bowed by age, continued to carry water up from the river, and while away his happy, carefree hours by telling of the brave days of old, when the world was young—had been consulted, he would have warned them that it was a year of portent for Fort Langley.

All of the old people knew that four was a mystical number, and sixteen was fraught with tremendous possibilities; it was four times sixteen summers since the white-crested floating island of Captain George Vancouver had been seen off the entrance of Stalo. It had been just sixteen years after Vancouver that Simon Fraser came, changing the name of the

Stalo to his own; and sixteen years later the great fire had wiped out the second fort. Now the cycle of four fours was again complete. Douglas knew that something had happened that might affect the whole land. Gold had been found!

It was first located on the Mainland—for there had been a brief excitement on Queen Charlotte Islands several years before—on the British side of the line north of Fort Colvile. Prospectors from Oregon stampeded there, and then made their way here and there, panning and testing creek bars. The Indians soon learned the value of the yellow metal. So it was, that writing to the Colonial office, London, October 29, 1856, Douglas said: "From successful experiments made in washing gold from the sands of the tributary streams of Fraser River, there is reason to suppose that the gold region is extensive."

A year later he reported:

> Concerning the goldfields of the Interior, north of 49 degree parallel, which for the sake of brevity, I will hereafter speak of as the 'Couteau Mines' (so named after the tribe of Indians who inhabit the country) I have received further intelligence from my correspondents in that quarter.
>
> It appears from their reports that the auriferous character is becoming daily more extensively developed, through the exertions of the native Indian tribes, who, having tested the sweets of gold finding are devoting much of their time and attention to that pursuit.
>
> The reputed wealth of the Couteau Mines is causing much excitement among the population of the United States territory of Washington and Oregon, and I have no doubt that a great number of people from those territories will be attracted thither with the return of the fine weather in Spring.

Douglas did not like the prospect; neither did Yale. They feared a collision between gold-mad miners and Indians. War had been raging for some time between natives and whites in Washington territory. The Chief Factor discussed the matter with Yale, and as a result he hurried to Nanaimo and persuaded Allard to return to the Fraser to reopen Fort Yale, which was bound to become a focal point in any gold excitement. Allard agreed to do so, provided that Fort Yale was no longer considered a subsidiary of Fort Langley. Years had done nothing to heal the breach between the former friends.

Douglas had expected, "a great number" would come, but he had no conception how great that number would be. Captain Jones of the schooner *Wild Pigeon* gave confirmation to the wild rumors that had percolated to the settlements ringing Puget Sound. The *Puget Sound Herald*, published at Steilacoom, Oregon Territory, reported on March 26, 1858 that Captain Jones had declared men were making from $8 to $50 a day, and that a man returning from Fort Langley had advised his friends to "come soon."

Within a matter of days the coal mines at Bellingham were idle, as the men had all crossed the border to the new diggings. Workers quit the mills. Large sailing vessels at Port Gable were abandoned by their crews who joined in the stampede. Soldiers deserted from the forts on the Sound. Farmers left their ploughing uncompleted to take their shovels and start off. And so the story went: 300 men were billeted in a bowling alley at Port Townsend on the way to the mines; Steilacoom was crowded, while Bellingham and Whatcom were sending off parties nearly every day. A trail had been commenced from Whatcom to join the brigade trail to Fort Hope.

They came in hundreds, and the hundreds became thousands. A veritable tidal wave of red-shirted, bearded men splashed down upon the banks of the Fraser. They eddied and swirled about Fort Langley, crowding the square and standing in line to buy supplies. Indians, Kanakas, halfbreeds and Europeans were questioned from morning until late at night: "What was the best place to prospect?" "How were the Indians?" "How far was it to the diggings?" "What were the latest reports on actual discoveries?" A jovial, good-natured and eager lot they were as they poured their money across the counters in such volume that for the first weeks of the rush sales averaged $1,500 daily.

Then came the thousands from San Francisco. They came in crazy old craft of every description, steamers, sailing vessels, river boats; crowded so tightly that men stood all the way for want of seats and lay in turn on the decks to doze. California had gone mad with excitement. Stories that had been magnified in the telling on Puget Sound were enlarged again and again by the time that they were repeated in the state that had its own great day of gold. For instance, it was said on the Sound that the Hudson's Bay Company had shipped away 110 pounds of gold! When this story was printed in San Francisco, it was more than 200 pounds that had been forwarded to London.

Douglas did not welcome the Californians. In this he was seconded by the Puget Sound communities. The *Herald* commenting, under date of May 7, in respect of their fellow Americans: "San Francisco is casting upon our shores thousands who can find no employment there, while from Oregon the cry is 'Still they come.' The free-lunch tables of San Francisco we fear, will soon be utterly abandoned, and the vendors of bad whiskey compelled to shut up shop." Hard words, indeed, but Douglas had heard even worse words about these new arrivals. He wrote

London that: "They are represented as being, with some exceptions a specimen of the worst of the population of San Francisco; the very dregs, in fact, of society. Their conduct here would have led me to form a very different conclusion." He was to learn that the exceptions were not the decent, hard working miners, but the worthless proportion that takes part in every migration.

Alarmed in 1858 at the totally unexpected size of the rush—it has been computed that there were as many as 30,000 adventurers who crowded into a territory where there were not more than 500 or 600 whites, in the space of three months—Douglas asked the Imperial government to set up authority, and to send out police and soldiers to keep the horde in order. In the meantime he took a desperate step; one that a less courageous man would have hesitated to do. He assumed control and appointed officers to act for the Crown. He had no authority to do so. His commissions only extended to Vancouver Island and the Queen Charlotte Islands. But he was fearful of what would happen if the stampeders were not held under some restraint.

He felt, too, that it was of utmost importance to obtain an acknowledgment of British sovereignty from all who entered the country. In order to do this, as early as 1859 he had taken the remarkable step of collecting a mining license from every one in the name of Queen Victoria. If, however, he argued, this action on his part was not sustained by law, then the only authority that could exist was that of the Hudson's Bay Company under its license of exclusive trade. And so he exacted a head tax in addition to the mining license. In this manner they acknowledged British authority through the great trading company.

While Douglas worried and fretted and took bold measures, the miners made their way up the river in their hundreds and thousands; they fought against the currents in leaky canoes, in home-made boats, in sailing craft and even on rafts; they crossed the portage from the Nicomekl—now covered by Fort Langley farms—and crowded about the post. The fields were white with tents, while along the edge of the woods were scores of cedar-bark shelters.

And by now gold was trickling down from the bars above Fort Hope. Douglas, who was at Fort Langley late in May, reported that he had heard of three men taking out 190 ounces of gold in seven days; of men making from $8 to $12 on the average; and of the rich discovery made on Hill's Bar, below Fort Yale, where as high as $25 a day was being taken. He found, too, that the affairs of the Company were being seriously disrupted; that Indians were being paid $2, $3 and $4 a day for working for the miners, and that none could be hired for the Company's service.

The rush was on in earnest, and the auriferous character of the country was established. Between February 18 and May 24, he found Fort Langley had accumulated, in addition to specie, no less than 648 ounces of gold. He went up the river and met the miners. Before leaving Fort Langley he had been interviewed by a number of men who wished to take up land. Here was a new problem. He wished to see them raising their own food if the rush was to be developed into a permanent mining industry. But he had no authority to grant them lands. All he could do was to refer the question to London.

Now he learned that the miners were pushing their adventurous way upstream beyond the canyons of the Fraser; higher and higher up the river they progressed, finding the bars richer and the gold coarser. This pointed to a great danger. If these men were caught by the winter snows the results might be tragic. A new road to the Interior must be built. Where was the money to come from? It was a puzzle, but not for long, the volunteer governor was equal to the occasion.

He induced some 500 miners to agree to work for nothing; further he persuaded them to put up $25 each as a guarantee of good conduct. This provided money for immediate requirements. This bond money was to be returned later, not in cash but in supplies. He recalled Anderson's exploration of the way between Cayoosh Creek and Harrison Lake. He sent for that hardy pathfinder and asked him to take charge of the laying out of the freight road by that route. He divided the men into companies under captains and set them to work. They started in July 1858 and freight was rolling into Lillooet on the Fraser in November. The situation had been saved; the danger averted, and mining placed on a more definite and permanent basis.

10

Fort Langley's Mightiest Moment

The summer of 1858 was one of excitement and confusion at Fort Langley. It was also one of changes, and these augured ill for the future prosperity of the old establishment.

Steam, applied to marine transportation, had anchored the post to the Fraser River in 1836, when the *Beaver* paddled bravely up the stream, making the journey in a few hours— one that often required days for sailing craft to accomplish. No attempt had been made to take mechanically propelled vessels beyond the fort. Now, however, daring Yankee skippers adventured higher up the Fraser and had reached Fort Hope, and later were to carry freight and passengers to Fort Yale at the very foot of the ramparts of the Coast Mountains. Soon steamers that formerly landed their cargoes and human freight at Fort Langley were making that place only a port of call. Others plied between the fort and the upper communities.

Naturally the larger vessels of deep draught, such as the HBC's *Beaver* and *Otter*, still recognized Fort Langley as the limit of safe navigation. And fortunate were the miners that the old trading concern had vessels to go even that length, for the Company fought strenuously against inflation. Although the trading vessels were required elsewhere, the Board of Management put them on the Victoria to Fraser River service when freight rates from Vancouver Island to Fort Yale sky-rocketed to $50 a ton.

The result was that the rates from Victoria to Fort Langley were forced down by the Company to $12 a ton. But the astute and greedy American captains plying the river beyond Fort Langley, met the situation by raising their tariff to $40 a ton, making the total, if the Hudson's Bay boats were used, higher by $2 than the direct charge by other craft.

Still the volume of trade to Fort Langley continued fairly heavy, but a decline had set in with the opening of navigation to Fort Hope. The American steamer *Surprise* was the first to make the trip. Speel-set, a Fort Langley Indian, had been secured by the steamer's captain to act as pilot, and August Willing, a clerk, went along as interpreter. The attempt was successful, and with the return of the *Surprise* to Fort Langley, the blanketted Indian had disappeared and a natty figure arrayed in a uniform of pilot cloth and brass buttons, and wearing a large panama hat and polished shoes stepped ashore. It was not Speel-set—for he had discarded the name. He was now "Captain John" and his pockets bulged with twenty shining five-dollar gold pieces. In other days one or two blankets would have been adequate payment for such a service.

Contact with white miners had not been so profitable to all Indians. Too many rough characters had regarded the natives with contempt that they made no effort to conceal. The inevitable clash took place, just as Douglas had feared it would, when he induced Allard to return to Fort Yale.

Word was carried to Fort Langley one day in late July that a white woman was being held prisoner by the Indians near the site of the old village of Skaiametl. She had been wounded and several white men had been killed by the natives, it was reported. Yale at once outfitted 45 men with muskets and revolvers and sent them to rescue the woman.

The Indians had been restless for weeks before this outbreak, right from the mouth of the river. Bodies floating out to sea were ascribed to Indian treachery.

It was a short, sharp war in the canyons above Yale, and many whites and Indians died—how many will never be definitely known. The more timid from the upriver communities dropped back on Fort Langley, but several hundreds of courageous miners formed themselves into armed companies and carried the fight to the natives. Peace was at last restored.

Yale had difficulty in accommodating himself to the changing conditions. Everything was different; even his old friend Chief Factor Douglas, now Governor James Douglas. The great man had always surrounded himself with a certain amount of impressive dignity; now he travelled with a military escort when he came to the Fraser River. He was attended by officers and men drawn from the Boundary Commission escort or by marines and seamen from the navy.

The economy in the establishment was once well regulated and orderly. Now it was sadly disrupted. Shacks of squatters spread along the river bank and on the broad flats. Whisky pedlars plied their trade with Indians and whites alike. Smuggling was becoming a regular calling.

Every time that Douglas appeared he was beseiged by land-hungry men. He could do nothing until government was established. He knew that a new colony was to be formed—and he was also aware that he was to be governor of it. He knew, too, that a military force would be available to him, for a specially selected Royal Engineers corps was to be sent out. He was informed about these things when, on September 15, he arrived at Fort Langley on a tour of inspection.

Here he was amazed to find that a group of ambitious speculators in Victoria had taken possession of the original fort and were subdividing it into lots, to be sold as being "in the town of Derby." He was furious, and issued a proclamation just as quickly as he could pen it. He declared that no land had been sold to any person, and that the affair was a swindle. He went to greater length: he formally took over the properties for the Crown, and sent Vancouver Island's Surveyor-General, Joseph Despard Pemberton, to check up on the surveys and make arrangements for selling lots to the public by auction.

Thus, it was speculators who first located Derby. Douglas was much impressed by their selection of the site for a town, for he found that it was favorably regarded by business men of Victoria.

The bill creating a new colony was passed in August 1858, Queen Victoria personally selecting the name, "British Columbia." Immediately two small detachments of Royal Engineers were despatched from England, Colonel Richard Clement Moody, with additional personnel following at intervals.

The Home Government also appointed Matthew Baillie Begbie, a tall young barrister of courage and determination as judge of the new colony, and Chartres Brew, formerly an officer of the Irish Constabulary, to organize a police force.

The first units of the Royal Engineers arrived within a short time of each other under Captain R. M. Parsons and Captain J. M. Grant. Brew came next and on November 15 Judge Begbie reached Victoria—and just in time, for Douglas had set November 19 as the great day upon which the Crown Colony of British Columbia would be proclaimed.

It was fitting, indeed, that the birth of a new colony should be celebrated at Fort Langley, and that there the inauguration of government by the Crown should take place, for Fort Langley had been a mighty instrument, fashioned by the old trading company, that had been a bulwark of British sovereignty on the North American continent—holding the Union Jack north of the 49th parallel.

Douglas planned to have an impressive ceremony in the fort square, with all possible pomp and dignity. But that morning was cold and miserable, with a constant drizzle of rain. The HBC's red ensign—that had flown so proudly and defiantly over the Fraser since that other November day, when Annance, the scholar, had unfurled it at the behest of James McMillan—hung limp and sodden as if in mourning for the completion of an age.

And it was just that, for later in the day, after James Douglas had officially taken office and added that of "His Excellency the Governor of British Columbia" to his other titles, he read a proclamation ending the license of exclusive trade of the Hudson's Bay Company.

But let the central figure in the pageant of the day tell the chronology of bringing into being government on the Mainland, as he did in a dispatch to Sir Edward Bulwer Lytton, Colonial Secretary:

> I proceeded on the 16th inst., by H.M.Ship Sattelite to Point Roberts and from thence by the Hudson's Bay Company's steamers Otter and Beaver to Fort Langley to proclaim the Act of Parliament providing for the Government of British Columbia.

> I was kindly accompanied on that occasion by Rear Admiral Maynes, by Mr. Cameron, Chief Justice of Vancouver's Island, and Mr. Begbie, the Judge of British Columbia, who arrived from San Francisco on the evening of the 15th inst., just in time to take part in the solemnity.

> Captain Parsons with the 1st Detachment of Royal Engineers also accompanied me from this place. Captain Grant with the Second Detachment, and also Inspector Brew having preceeded me by a few days.

> The ceremony was performed at Fort Langley with becoming solemnity, on the 19th inst., in the presence of those gentlemen, Her Majesty's troops and the inhabitants of the place and the officers holding appointments from Her Majesty were installed in the usual manner, and with the accustomed forms.

> Proclamations were then made:

> 1. Of the revocation by Her Majesty of all the exclusive privileges of the Hudson's Bay Company. 2. Indemnifying the officers of Government from all irregularities previous to the proclamation of the act. 3. Proclaiming English Law to be the Law of the Colony.

> Copies of these proclamations are herewith transmitted for the information of Her Majesty's Government.
>
> I returned to this place on the 21st instant, and Rear Admiral Baynes and all the other Gentlemen who accompanied me to Fort Langley except Captains Grant and Parsons, who were left with the Royal Engineers at old Fort Langley.

Such was the manner in which Douglas described Fort Langley's mightiest moment, when government was born in the big room in the Big House within the stockade. He had first officiated as Governor of Vancouver Island in inducting Begbie into office, and then the big heavy-bearded barrister, who had been a Justice of the Supreme Court for a matter of minutes, administered the customary oaths to James Douglas, who thereupon was officially and legally the governor—and government—of British Columbia.

And then the men who had been carrying on as government officers and Chartres Brew, the talented police officer, were installed. The officials who formally entered upon their now lawful duties and who had been indemnified for their actions in office to that moment, included: Richard Hicks, revenue officer and assistant gold commissioner at Yale; Robert Smith, holding similar appointments at Fort Hope; George Perrier, justice of the peace at Hill's Bar; P. B. Whannell, magistrate at Yale; W. H. Ladner, police chief at Fort Hope; W. H. Bevis, revenue officer at Fort Langley, and O. T. Travaillot, assistant gold commissioner at the Forks of the Fraser (Lytton).

And while these ceremonies were being celebrated with as much pomp and circumstance as the crowded big room of the officers' quarter would permit, and with salutes fired in the rain, the rest of British Columbia and Vancouver Island were without realization of the significant character of the happenings with the fort.

"As the first day of the existence of a new colony destined to occupy no unimportant place in the history of the future," the San Francisco *Evening Bulletin*, December 9, commented, "the nineteenth of November might have been, very properly, considered a fit occasion for burning gunpowder, etc.; but everything was quiet here (Victoria), in fact, few knew anything about it until the announcement was published in the Gazette."

It was a proud day for His Excellency Governor James Douglas, but a bitter one for the man who had been associated with the Hudson's Bay Company in the days when the towering Douglas was an apprentice with the North West Company. And as he listened, from an inconspicuous place to the reading of the revocation of the Hudson's Bay Company's privileges, Yale could not help but recall how that concern had come to the Fraser delta when there was doubt as to what country would eventually control the Columbia, and of how it had been destined as a depot for the Interior; and of how he had given the best that was in him for thirty years to build the fort and district into one of the leading ones in the West, and of how he had fought the Clallam and the Yuculta to protect it…and now, his world was finally crashing about him.

He was not opposed to ordered government, but he was human, and Fort Langley was his, and he was of the Company. And so it was that Yale asked for a holiday: he had not had one for years. He wanted to get away from it all, needed time to think.

Now Governor Douglas, of British Columbia, could issue land titles. So, without loss of time, the sale of lots at Derby was held in Victoria. Pemberton was the auctioneer. It was planned to hold the sale within the public offices of Vancouver Island, but such was the crowd that turned up to bid against one another for property, that proceedings, on the first day, had to be conducted outside. Lots had an upset price of $100, and Pemberton explained that he would not take less. He did not expect more. The Victoria correspondent of the *Bulletin*, attended on the opening day, November 25, and described the scene in that paper, 9 December:

> The bidding commenced at once very briskly. The prices offered seemed to astonish many, and particularly the auctioneer, who used no effort to obtain a higher price, but in fact seemed amazed. Evidently he was unused to such a crowd, and such a way of 'going it blind', and 'taking the chances', and seemed to think them great fools to pay so much when they only asked $100.

> Lots brought as high as $750. I witnessed the sale of the first twenty lots, which averaged $355. They sold, the first day, 205 lots, for over $41,000. The sale continued for three days.

> Buildings will commence going up at Langley at once. The Government advertises for proposals for building a church, parsonage, court house and jail. Various parties have purchased lumber here, to take there, to build stores and houses.

The action of Douglas in sanctioning this sale is hard to understand, for two days before he was sworn in as governor, Captain Grant had written to him, warning him against such a thing. In a survey of the situation, of remarkable clarity, Captain Grant had pointed out that he was addressing the governor-to-be "with a view of delaying the sale of any land which will tend to establish a town without fuller information being obtained."

He objected to the site of the proposed town for several reasons. It was hard to defend; it was open to smuggling from the United States, and while steamers could reach it, the prevailing winds did not always allow sailing craft to do so with ease and despatch. He favored locating the chief town at the confluence of the Pitt and Fraser, where the slopes of Mary Hill, the deep water, and winds and ease of protection, commended themselves for such a project.

Douglas was accustomed to giving orders, not to taking advice that might be regarded as criticism of his actions. He ignored Grant, but he could not so readily brush aside similar suggestions coming from Colonel Moody, who arrived on Christmas Day, for Moody held a commission as Chief Commissioner of Works, and dormant authority as lieutenant-governor. Moreover, he had powerful friends in London.

So, with what grace he could muster, Douglas agreed to Moody's recommendation that Grant's suggestions be followed. As a result, early in 1859 further surveys were made of the locality about Mary Hill, but Moody saw greater possibilities in building on the slopes of the first high land on the north side of the Fraser where there was a broad expanse of deep water. Here accommodation along the shore could be found for ships of the deepest draught that could possibly enter the river and so immediate preparations were made to build a camp there for the Royal Engineers.

These trained and efficient builders verified the wisdom of the earliest dwellers on Stalo—for they selected the old site of Skaiametl for their camp, which they named Sapperton, while the city they planned was Queenborough, later changed by Her Majesty Queen Victoria, to New Westminster.

While New Westminster took form and grew in importance, Fort Langley declined, while the town of fond hopes—Derby—withered. Disappointed purchasers were offered opportunity of buying in the new townsite and of applying payments to the purchase of lands there. Some availed themselves of the offer; others did not. Derby's barracks, and jail and other government buildings gradually disappeared, the lumber being used elsewhere. The church, some years later, was moved across the river to Maple Ridge, and the site of the town of Derby by 1947 was part of the farm of Alexander Houston.

And in the immediate years that followed, all the dangers that Captain Grant had anticipated were realized. Langley became the resort for many worthless characters. There were robberies, and other crimes reported to revenue officer Bevis, who kept his pen employed constantly in telling his troubles to the governor. There was also, he asserted, a regular trade being carried on in smuggling goods from the United States.

Then, too, when Peter O'Reilly replaced Bevis in 1859, he reported that the United States Army escort troops had camped on British soil; a soldier had stolen a gun from a saloon keeper near Semiahmoo Bay, who had followed him to the U.S. camp. The saloonkeeper, John Shaw, had been chased half a mile further into British territory, and had there been shot down by an army sergeant named Leonard. Judge Begbie became interested and told O'Reilly to make complaint to Leonard's superior officer. This was done, but the officer only replied with a bombastic speech.

The following year, an armed force under an officer crossed the boundary and invaded Langley, capturing two men, claiming they were deserters, and took them away. The *New Westminster Times*, (published in Victoria) February 2, 1860, tells the story:

> Information has just arrived that an American officer named McKibbon, marched with a sergeant's guard to Langley, and arrested there two men whom he claimed as prisoners, and took them over the boundary. He acted, he stated, by orders from his commanding officer, and was ready to resist any attack made upon him.

And while all these things were happening, Yale was wandering in the east, wondering and fretting where he could go, and what he would do; only to return to Victoria at last. He did not want to go back to Fort Langley, and had offered to accept a post in the Peace River district. But this soon lost its appeal.

He decided at last to purchase land near Victoria, where he could occasionally chat with his old friend John Tod, with Anderson the pathfinder, and John Work, the wise old Irishman, who had pioneered the way with McMillan from Puget Sound to the Stalo. So he bought land by the side of the Colquitz River, and he roamed about in the pleasant woods by day, but when night came, "reminiscences and sadness that none of my fondest hopes, though always seeming fair, have availed."

And these memories and saddened thoughts revolved about the stockades of Fort Langley and of the figures of men, white and dark, that played their parts in the pageantry of his mind. There was old Whattlekainum, and Shashia, the prince and diplomat, and Scanawa whose trading instincts had won him a fortune in white man's goods and lost him his life. There were Annance and Manson, and Archibald McDonald, with whom he had worked to devise additional production from both river and forests.

In those musings and rememberings, it was with pride that Yale recalled that Old Langley—his Langley—had been the first outpost of civilization on the British Columbia coast. It was there that the salmon fisheries had developed as an export industry; that native timber had been used to manufacture barrels and casks. It was from Langley's broad acres that much of the produce went to pay the leasehold requirements on the panhandle of Alaska; and the trade in cranberries, and isinglass.

Yale would recall, also, how only such a short time ago—but it seemed longer and far away—it had become the supply centre of the brigades; and there was the nightmare of the gold rush, when redshirted, bearded men had swarmed like grasshoppers over the land, bringing trouble and confusion with them; and then, too, it was as if only yesterday that British Columbia was born at Fort Langley.

Bruce Alastair McKelvie
The local historian as hero.

Denys Nelson, author of the first history of Fort Langley, wrote: "(by) 1863 HBC stations in the Lower Fraser Valley were: Fort Langley, in charge of W.H. Newton; Fort Hope, in charge of W. Charles; and Fort Yale, in charge of Ovid Allard."

There was little else to say. By 1864, Allard "was transferred to Fort Langley," which he'd left years earlier after his argument with his old friend, James Murray Yale. "The fort", continues Nelson, "was by this time being gradually dismantled. The front and part of the stockade were taken down by degrees between 1861 and 1864, and the remainder was allowed to fall into disrepair and not preserved. Its days as a fort were over.

"In 1872 the Big House, built in 1840, became quite unsafe. Allard made repeated representations to the Board of Management at Victoria, but nothing was done. Early in the year, Jason relates, Dr. W.F. Tolmie, the senior member of the board, paid a visit to the Fort. That night the wind rose to a hurricane, and the old house shook and groaned with the stress and buffering. The doctor, who sought the assistance and comfort of Allard, was assured that that was the usual thing to expect at Langley, and that the only really safe place was in the potato cellar, where, it is said, the doctor spent the remainder of the night.

"The order came soon afterwards to rebuild, which was done, the old house being removed and replaced by the building which was taken down in 1925. This was erected by William Cromarty, formerly foreman cooper at the fort." Ovid Allard died here in 1874, having served the Company for 40 years. His successor, William H. Newton, died a year later. In turn, Nelson tells us, there followed Henry Wark, nephew of John Work, of Murray's 1824 expedition; he served from 1875 to 1886. William Sinclair came next, and, like Wark, is listed as Postmaster in the HBC records. James M. Drummond, a clerk, was in charge from 1887 to 1892. From June 1892 to January 1893, Walter Wilkie ran what was left of the post. Frank Powell was the last man in charge, and he served until the post was closed, 26 June 1895.

Fort Langley's history comes to a close, as Bruce McKelvie realized so clearly, with the Fraser River gold rush of 1858. After this the Fort is only a bit player in a drama that includes the Cariboo gold rush, the construction and heyday of the Cariboo Road, the development of such nearby farming areas as Sumas and Chilliwack, and the growth of the Municipality of Fort Langley, which was incorporated on 26 April 1873.

"The arrival in the Valley," Denys Nelson observed, "of the Canadian Pacific Railway did nothing to help Langley, except, indirectly, through the opening of the Valley and the development of the province. The coming of the British Columbia Electric Interurban Railway in 1910 did still less, for it took away much of Fort Langley's previous trade, which had been largely carried on by shipping the farm produce down the Fraser River to New Westminster."

Writing not long after Denys Nelson, another of Fort Langley's historians observed: "Fort Langley of to-day is but a pretty country village. Its periods of pre-eminence have ceased. But it has its memories of the days when the industries of civilization in British Columbia took form and shape around it."

When the bronze tablet was unveiled at Fort Langley, 2 May 1925, C.H. French, head of the HBC's Pacific Coast fur department, said "it is a great pleasure to be with you to-day as the representative of the glorious old Company of Adventurers of England. Langley is a name that is destined to be handed down in history from generation to generation, carrying with it that spirit of adventure that goes with miners, fur traders, trappers and empire builders.

"It was here that the fur trader on the Coast first shook hands with the trappers. It was here that the fur traders grasped the hands of miners from California, and we cannot overlook the fact that while the fur trader opened up the country, pacified the natives and ensured British rule, the miner had a large share in effecting developments that would have taken many years to achieve had he not arrived.

"What wonderful men were these fur traders! The more one knows about them the more one wonders how it was possible to gather such picked men together at these remote spots. It took years to get supplies and for many years one mail each year was as much as could be expected. Ordinary wages would not do it."

Wondering about such questions as this one posed by C.H. French was, one knows, what kept Bruce McKelvie writing history. It is ironic, then, that his best book is about a place. He did, of course, use Fort Langley as a stage for his characters, but his belief that Fort Langley was the linchpin in British Columbia history kept him from straying from the Fort's story. Proof that he felt this strongly about Fort Langley can be found in two chapters of his *Early History of the Province of British Columbia* (1926). It's the focus of the action in one chapter of *Tales of Conflict* (1950); a good deal of the activity in *Pageant of B.C.* (n.d.) moves through Fort Langley; and the Fort plays a minor but colourful role in *The Black Canyon* (1927), one of McKelvie's novels.

It's in the Foreward to this novel that we find McKelvie quoting from the notes of Dr. Walkem, one of BC's earliest physicians: "Before starting mining they formed a company and elected officers, the foreman being Jack McLennan and the assistant foreman, Archie McDonald Jack McLennan was subsequently killed by the savages.

"After working for some time and getting nothing but fine gold, they started upstream in search of the motherlode. In the meantime men had been pouring into the country...so that when they left...they had no fear of the two men they had left in charge of their boats being murdered by the Indians who were beginning to be aggressive.

"While moving from place to place they met many Indians...who appeared to be quiet and peaceful. One young woman formed a strong attachment for Jack McLennan, who gave her clothing....She followed him about, insisting on carrying his pack. At night Jack insisted on her staying with her friends, who always followed the prospectors' trail.

"One night this young woman suddenly appeared and said in a subdued voice, 'Hist!...Before sun up you white men go. Go back in the stick (forests) far, far, far. Then go to saltchuck (the ocean). Indian kill all white men in canyon, by and by kill you all. Tomorrow he come. Go quick.' The young woman then disappeared as silently as she had come.

Afterwards, "passing from a small bench below Jackass Mountain to another bench the Indians, who were concealed in the brush, fired from above. Three of the miners were wounded....These men died the next day. Travelling was now continued during the night by this small band of miners, and when day broke they went into camp fortified by timber and brush....A man was lost every day and among these was Jack McLennan, and at Slaughter Bar six of the party were killed....As the miners were killed, their comrades threw the bodies into the Fraser...."

Little as this has to do with Fort Langley, it has much to do with McKelvie's view of history. Although subsequent historians have agreed with McKelvie's assessment of Fort Langley's role, they have not been so quick to sanction his approach and style. In the early 1950s McKelvie addressed the History Club at the University of British Columbia, where he proved an invigorating speaker who was as entertaining as he was knowledgeable, or so it seemed to one listener. But the next day one of the professors who had also been in the audience told his students that it didn't matter if what McKelvie said was right or wrong, what mattered was that it wasn't history.

This opinion—and it is only opinion—has persevered, spread, one imagines, by this professor's students, not by readers. McKelvie never lacked readers. During his long career his books remained popular, as did his countless magazine and newspaper articles. Today his books are difficult to locate and, when found, expensive—always a healthy sign.

But there is more to it than any one simple answer can explain away. In exploring McKelvie's situation, one cannot hope to make McKelvie acceptable to schoolmasters, nor can any brief sketch revitalize his professional reputation; what one can do, though, by putting McKelvie into perspective, is clarify one or two corners of the muddy pool that is BC history today.

In 1958, Walter N. Sage, a professor and one of BC's better-known mid-century historians, selected six of British Columbia's earliest historians. Needless-to-say McKelvie did not make the list; this may have been due to his youth, still, McKelvie was a near contemporary of at least one man who did make the list. The six were: H.H. Bancroft, Alexander Begg, Rev. A.G. Morice, O.M.I., R.E. Gosnell, E.O.S. Scholefield, and Judge F.W. Howay. As far as can be told, the work of these men was all out of print in 1958, and one or two of their histories may have been generally unavailable for half a century.

Now, thirty-three years after Professor Sage's selection, only Father Morice's *The History of the Northern Interior of British Columbia* (1904) remains in print in this province. The truth is that, with the exception of Bancroft (whose many books are reprinted frequently in the United States) and Morice, none of Sage's early historians can hold a reader's attention today. Even Judge Howay, exemplary historian though he surely was, fails to communicate. His audience during his life was fellow workers, today his audience is made up of historians, researchers, and students.

Outwardly McKelvie would seem to have fared little better. His novels are out of print; so are his historical works. Yet on closer inspection we find the story of his publication is more complicated than first glance would suggest. His three novels—*The Black Canyon* (1927), *Hulgowget* (1926), *Pelts and Powder* (1929)—required British and Canadian editions. *Early History of the Province of British Columbia* appears to have enjoyed a decent life as a school textbook in British Columbia. *Maquinna* (1946) and *Fort Langley* (1947) were reprinted twice; the same is true for *Tales of Conflict* (1949). McKelvie's *Pageant of B.C.* (1955) was republished in a "B.C. Centennial Edition" in 1957, and since has remained a popular library book. His last book, *Magic, Murder, and Mystery* (1966), posthumously published by McKelvie's son, may lack the authority of his early work but nothing is wrong with the writing.

As McKelvie seems to have written the blurb about himself for the Centennial Edition of *Pageant*, it is worth quoting; he seldom talked about himself so frankly. "Bruce Alistair McKelvie is fairly well convinced that his ancestors roamed the country north of the Tweed, but he is proud of the fact that he was born in British Columbia. He arrived in Vancouver only two years after the C.P.R.

"At the age of ten he started working as a printer's devil in a newspaper office—and has followed the newspaper calling ever since. During his boyhood he lived in different parts of the province and listened with avid interest to the stories told by the pioneers of the West Coast. He has never lost this interest in the colourful story of the Pacific Slope, and has had the unique honour of being acclaimed, by all the parties in the B.C. Legislature, 'the foremost historian of the Province'. In appreciation of his contribution to the knowledge of Western history, a high mountain on Vancouver Island was named Mount McKelvie, and a stream McKelvie Creek.

"His endeavour has been to present history in an interesting manner; to picture individuals and scenes as they existed, rather than to make them conform to stereotyped characters and incidents. The pageantry that he presents in this book is the result of forty years research."

More precisely, McKelvie was born 19 November 1889, educated in various BC locations, and began his journalism career in 1910. He wrote for the *Vancouver Province* and was, for seven years, managing editor of Victoria's *Colonist*. During his professional life, McKelvie was known as a top-ranking political reporter, though many thought his early work as a police reporter deserved equal billing. He was the only legislative reporter ever to sit in a cabinet meeting as an Indian chief. For saving the life of a young Indian girl on Texada Island, her father, himself a Sliammon chief, made the then ten-year-old Bruce McKelvie an honourary chief. Years later McKelvie joined an Indian delegation in the legislature to help them plead for better treatment.

Stories about "Pinkie" McKelvie are legion. Looking back, it's clear that McKelvie's biggest story was Brother XII. His exclusives in 1928 on the activities of this religious leader and fakir—active in and around the Nanaimo area in the late 1920s and early 1930s—made headlines across North America and Britain.

McKelvie himself was fascinated by nearly every aspect of British Columbia history, but he made the near-fatal mistake of, we may say, trying to serve God and Mammon too.

Early on McKelvie's contemporary and fellow British Columbian, Stewart H. Holbrook, realized that writing was a full- time career, so he left the BC logging camps behind and moved to Portland, Oregon. If Holbrook did not know how to write, he did know what a U.S. market meant. There Holbrook continued his varied career (among other things he'd been a journalist and vaudevillian), this time in a variety of editorial positions for logging newspapers and magazines. Up to this point, the mid-twenties, Holbrook and McKelvie's careers can hardly be compared; and four or five years later their careers could hardly have been more dissimilar: Holbrook was still teaching himself how to write while McKelvie was a successful journalist, historian and author of a competent BC history for the school system, and author of three novels.

Ten years later the picture was completely reversed. McKelvie had published no more books, while Holbrook had gone on to write *Holy Old Mackinaw: A Natural History of the American Lumberjack*, which remains, fifty years after its original publication, one of the most popular books of its type written in North America. Holbrook had also written a book on the American iron and steel industry, another on a revolutionary war hero, and within a year or two he'd begin collecting his occasional journalism in such long-popular books as *Lost Men of American History* and *Murder Out Yonder: An Informal Study of Certain Classic Crimes in Back-Country America*.

Holbrook would continue publishing, nineteen more books before his death in 1964, and cut himself out a career as a prolific and popular historian and writer. McKelvie did not publish a book between 1929 and 1947. Various reasons can be given for his virtual demise as a historian and writer, the nearest at hand being that he was busy with his career, running for public offices, and raising a family. But Holbrook raised a family, wrote a tremendous amount of journalism for a living—but no matter: what made Holbrook a success and crippled McKelvie was geography not psychology.

Oregon history, different as it may be from the past as it's known in the east and northeast, remains US history. Themes such as logging, murder, pioneer life, great men and small, all belong to the larger picture of the United States, because they have eastern parallels. Not so in British Columbia and Canada. Our history, or at least our history up to and through the 1858 gold rush on the Fraser River, the period about which McKelvie took a lasting interest, is more closely linked to that of the Pacific Northwest and southeastern Alaska.

Readers of the earlier sections of this book will have already noted that Fort Langley's story begins within the palisades of Fort Astoria and Fort Vancouver, both on the Columbia River. HBC concerns are the links connecting Fort Langley to the world beyond the Pacific Slope. The leasing of the Alaska Panhandle binds Fort Langley to Sitka and Moscow, just as a few years later the gold rush will strengthen the links, first created by trade, with California. Only when disappointed prospectors from eastern Canada, the majority of whom reached their new homesteads via California, begin settling on the floodlands of the Lower Fraser does British Columbia's north-south axis begin to shift east-west.

Thus the second stage (1808-1858) of BC's European history, the first being its overlapping but strictly maritime (1774-1820) fur trading period, is an early chapter, and then a continuation of Northwest Coast history, i.e. the history of the Pacific Slope from San Francisco north to the Bering Sea. To look at it otherwise is to confuse the issue, but that's exactly what McKelvie did.

Being a good Canadian, or a good British Columbia, is not necessarily the criteria for a good historian. North American nationalism, as recent Canadian history has proven, rarely has an objective; it simply feeds on itself. It is equally true that writing must have an objective. Although Bruce McKelvie's love of Canada and British Columbia is easily understood, the virtual demise of McKelvie as an author and historian during this period is not so easily understood unless we realize Stewart H. Holbrook had an ever-increasing audience, for the U.S. was growing by leaps and bounds in the 1920s and 1930s. North of the border, McKelvie's audience was shrinking. The older generation of British Columbians interested in the past was rapidly being outnumbered by a generation interested only in the future. Still, in spite of the odds, McKelvie wrote some of BC's finest non-academic narrative history; what Holbrook described, speaking of his own work, as "low brow" history.

Writers do not thrive in isolation; few, in fact, emerge from the critical silence of family and friends, and though there certainly are exceptions, McKelvie is not one of them. Compounding his isolation as a writer were other factors no less stulifying: there was no publishing industry in BC during his life, fewer magazines than today, less than half-a-dozen book stores, and one fledgling university. So, while it is right to say McKelvie's heart ruled his mind it is just as fair to say had his enthusiasm not been tempered by distance, McKelvie would have become Canada's Bernard DeVoto or, ignoring gender, Mari Sandoz. But stuck in the here and now we must appreciate the fact that the man stayed on Vancouver Island and became Bruce McKelvie.

No one knows how much work he produced. He was a prolific journalist writing for provincial, national and international newspapers and magazines. Then there are the books and pamphlets, among the latter are two little-known works: *Legends of Stanley Park* (n.d.) and *HBC in BC* (1958). There is no record of his contributions to books edited by others.

What provides an ongoing allure to anyone who bothers to read his or her way through McKelvie's books is their accuracy, whether fact or fiction, and books like *Maquinna* are something of both. But in the case of *Fort Langley* there is no reason to believe that anything was fictionalized, though McKelvie did some educated guessing—but, what historian has not done the same in his time?

In his notes to Chapter One, McKelvie used the then-available modern spelling of Indian names, and he "made an effort to identify some geographical locations, such as New Westminster with the names used by the Indians." In this edition names have again been modernized, wherever possible. There is no reason to check the accuracy of the Indian stories, such as the arrival and activities of Simon Fraser and his men. McKelvie based his narrative on the stories told by Jason Ovid Allard, who was born at Fort Langley in 1848. Allard was, wrote McKelvie, "possessed of a very retentive memory. He wrote fluently and with a beautiful hand, and present-day knowledge of much of the romance and lore of the development of the pioneer establishment is due to him."

The story of the *Tonquin* disaster as told by Tent-a-coose in Chapter Two is open to question. There is no material evidence that the *Tonquin* was blown up on Vancouver Island's west coast, rather the existing evidence suggests it was attacked and destroyed somewhere near Cape Sutil on the northern end of the island. The ship's last anchorage will likely remain one of the coast's many unsolved and, perhaps, unsolvable mysteries.

Later in his notes to Chapter Two, McKelvie quoted the Instrument of Restoration, the formal return of Astoria to the United States on 6 October 1818. A more important event took place on 20 October of that year, Britain and the United States signed the London Convention. This agreement, among other things, "provisionally set the 49th parallel as the boundary" between the US and what is today Canada, a line that stretched from the Rockies east to the Lake of the Woods.

Because the focus of this book switches from Fort Astoria to the Fraser River and Fort Langley at this point, the following passages from *Silliman's Magazine*, 1834, are worth quoting: "The North West Company did not enjoy the sway they had acquired over the trading region of the Columbia. A competition, ruinous in its expenses, which had long existed between them and the Hudson's Bay Company, ended in their downfall and the ruin of most of the partners. The relics of the company became merged in the rival association, and the whole business was conducted under the name of the Hudson's Bay Company.

"This coalition took place in 1821. They then abandoned Astoria, and built a large establishment sixty miles up the river, on the right bank, which they called Fort Vancouver. This was in a neighborhood where provisions could be more readily procured, and where there was less danger from molestation by any naval force. The company are said to carry on an active and prosperous trade, and to give great encouragement to settlers. They are extremely jealous, however, of any interference or participation in their trade, and monopolize it from the coast of the Pacific to the mountains, and for a considerable extent north to south."

The idea that the Americans drove the HBC out of Oregon is an old one among Canadians, but it seems that British politicians and HBC officials, such as George Simpson, knew that the London Convention had rung the death knell for the HBC on the Columbia. After that it was only a matter of time. And the final peal did not ring in 1846, when the HBC lost its territory south of the 49th parallel, nor did the bells ring one final time in 1871 when the HBC closed its last post in Oregon. The last peal rang in the 1880s when the US government paid the HBC $650,000 in gold bullion for its losses.

Concerning names introduced in chapters three, four, and five, McKelvie has this to say: "The crossing between the Nicomekl and Salmon rivers, across the flat lands of what is now Langley Prairie, was named by the Indians T'salkwaskyan. The same name was applied to the Salmon River, so the whole route became known as such. The trail from the fort to the farm was not developed for some years, transport to and from the farm being effected by flat bottomed boats on the winding, twisting, languid Salmon."

The Little River mentioned in chapters Three and Five is today's Kanaka Creek, named to commemorate the Kanaka—Hawaiian—labourers, who served the HBC so loyally. The Indians built a village on its shores after they moved away from Skaiametl; here the northern Indians that McKelvie calls the Yuculta were finally defeated, and there coal was found by James Murray Yale.

Thomas Langley, who inherited his brother's HBC stock in 1783, was a company director from 1800 to 1830.

"No further records," writes McKelvie, "have been found that might suggest the surname of the first baby born at Fort Langley. The fact that its first Christian name was 'Louis' might indicate that such was in compliment to his father, but there were at least two men stationed there in 1828 who bore that name. Some twenty years later the son of one of those men committed suicide when he was upbraided for marrying an aged squaw, so, perhaps, it is just as well that positive identification cannot be made."

The victory over the northern Indians described in Chapter Six is "an outstanding incident of Indian warfare" on BC's west coast. "It is not only detailed in the Fort journal, but is related by the storytellers of the Kwantlen, with comparative accuracy. It is the general correctness of Indian narration of historical events, which may be substantiated, that makes it possible to place dependence upon the account of subsequent wiping out of the Yuculta fleet that came to attack the village opposite the fort in 1837. There are no known reports from Fort Langley covering that period. Old-time residents and clergymen, who have ministered to the Kwantlen for many years, have no doubt as to the slaughter occasioned upon that momentous day."

Subsequent research has proved that the second and third Fort Langleys (1839-1896) were located at almost identical sites some 4km up river from the mouth of the Salmon River; the first fort (1827-1839) was located 2.3km below the mouth of the Salmon.

Father Demers's visit to Fort Langley "marks a starting point in the religious history of the province. It is true that the Spanish priests ministered 'to the people of the west coast of Vancouver Island in the 1790s, but Father Demers ' commenced the teaching of the Christian faith on a basis that has been continuous."

No one will ever agree on certain details regarding the gold rush to the bars of the Fraser River. Too much happened too quickly. "In 1903," McKelvie tells us, "Hon. Richard McBride, Provincial secretary, became convinced, as a result of personal inquiry, that the nearest that any one person could be identified with the first discovery of the gold that was the immediate cause of the rush of 1857-58 was James Houston, who wandered across the border where he was prospecting, and where his partner was killed by Indians, and found gold at Tranquille Creek near Kamloops. Houston later took up land covering the site of the original Fort Langley. He died in 1903 just as recognition was about to be given him".

The townsite of Derby, "the first subdivided property placed on the market, and the site of the original Fort Langley, is often referred to as the 'First capital of British Columbia.' There is no official confirmation for this belief. Another misconception is that there was no objection to its being developed until the arrival of Colonel R.C. Moody, who reached Victoria on Christmas Day. Actually Captain Grant of the Royal Engineers put his objections in writing and submitted them to Douglas before the Crown Colony was proclaimed. There is plenty of evidence that it was the hope and intention of Douglas to make Derby—or as he usually referred to it, 'Old Langley'—a large town, and he intended to have the Royal Engineers located there. There is no indication that the Governor ever intended for it to be the political capital of the colony."

With the addition of these notes Bruce McKelvie made his study of Fort Langley one of British Columbia's few interesting and trustworthy local history sketches. Locally it belongs alongside Peter C. Newman's *Company of Adventurers* and *Caesars of the Wilderness*—books proving that readability is important, that history does not belong to the few, and that narrative power is not a literary vice.

An editor faces few choices when dealing with a book such as *Fort Langley*. Reprinting it as is may be a well-intentioned idea, but it lacks merit for several reasons. First, enough research has been done since the 1947 to warrant this material being incorporated into the text, wherever feasible. Then there are the numerous small glitches in the text that should be corrected, snags that range from typos to a few stylistic excesses. New editions should be as contemporary as are translations, and as up-to-date as a map.

When Bruce McKelvie died in 1960 British Columbia was on the verge of a revolution. Had he lived another decade, he would have witnessed the birth and death of dozens of literary magazines; the creation of several national and international-class magazines that are still going strong; and half a dozen publishing houses. During these years book stores sprang up everywhere. And, what McKelvie might have found most amazing of all, there began developing a wide-spread interest in, and desire to write, local history.

Had McKelvie lived into the 1970s and continued to write, like Hubert Evans—a novelist only four years his junior—who became an elder for many Canadian writers in the 1970s, McKelvie would undoubtedly have become a seminal figure for local historians such as Derek Pethick, a professional author of still-unappreciated dimensions.

As it is, McKelvie lived to see none of this. And those of us who wish we had met him also wish he was still around to help us. All the evidence suggests that no one, before or since, has known move about the writing of British Columbia history than Bruce Alastair McKelvie.

Bibliography

Please note the following abbreviations are used below: BCARS (British Columbia Archives and Records Service), BCHQ (British Columbia Historical Quarterly) and WHQ (Washington Historical Quarterly).

Allard, J.O. Reminiscences. BCARS.

Anderson, A.C. History of the Northwest Coast. BCARS.
Journal of an Expedition..., BCARS.

Baker, Burt Brown. *Letters of Dr. John McLoughlin*. 1948.

Bancroft, H.H. *History of British Columbia*. 1887.
History of the Northwest Coast. 1884.

Begbie, M.B. Correspondence with Governor James Douglas. BCARS.

Corney, Peter. *Early Voyages in the North Pacific*. 1965.

Cox, Ross. *Adventures on the Columbia River*. 1831.

Creech, E.P. "Similkameen Trails, 1846-61". BCHQ. 1941.

Demers, Modeste. Report of Mission to Fraser River, *Diocese of Quebec Mission Reports*. 1843.

Douglas, James. Papers, BCARS.

Duff, Wilson. *The Upper Stalo Indians*. 1952.

Dye, E.E. *McLoughlin and Old Oregon*. 1900.

Elliott, T.C. "Journal of John Work". WHQ. July 1912.

Ermatinger, Francis. Journal of Clallum Expedition, 1828. BCARS.

Franchere, Gabriel. *Voyage to the Northwest Coast of America*. 1954.

Fraser, Simon. *The Letters & Journals of Simon Fraser, 1806-1808*. 1960.

Grant, J.M. Letter to Governor Douglas, Nov. 17, 1858. BCARS.

Great Britian. Papers Relative to Affairs of British Columbia. BCARS.

Green, George. *History of Burnaby and Vincinity.* 1947.

Hazlitt, W.C. *British Columbia and Vancouver Island*. 1858.

Helmcken, J.S. *The Reminiscences of Doctor John Sebastian Helmcken*. 1975.

Hill-Tout, Charles. *The Salish People*. Talon Books. 1978.

Howay, F.W. *The Work of the Royal Engineers in British Columbia*. 1910.
   The Early History of the Fraser River Mines. 1926.

Landerholm, Carl. *Notices and Voyages of the Famed Quebec Mission*.1956.

Langley, Fort. Journal, 1827-1830. BCARS.
   "Fort Langley Correspondence". BCHQ. July 1937.

McDonald, Archibald. *Peace River*. 1872.

Macfie, Matthew. *Vancouver Island and British Columbia*. 1865.

McLeod, John, Sr. Correspondence, 1812-1844. BCARS.

McLoughlin, John. *Letters from Fort Vancouver*. 1941-1944.

Manson, Mrs. Aurelia. Reminiscences. BCARS.

Mayne, R.C. *Four Years in British Columbia and Vancouver Island*. 1862.

Meany, E.S. *History of the State of Washington*. 1909.

Merk, Frederick. *Fur Trade and Empire*. 1931.

Moody, R.C. Correspondence with Governor Douglas. BCARS.

Murphy, Paul. History of Fort Langley. 1929. location unknown.

National Parks Canada. *Fort Langley.* 1961.

Nelson, Denys. *Fort Langley, 1827-1927*. 1927.
   Place Names of the Delta of the Fraser. BCARS.

Newman, Peter C. *Caesars of the Wilderness*. 1987.

Newspapers;
   Evening Bulletin (San Francisco).
   Puget Sound Herald.
   British Colonist.
   Victoria Gazette.
   Le Courrier de la Nouvelle Caledonie (Victoria).
   New Westminister Times.

Parks Canada *Fort Langley National Park*. n.d.

Peers, H.N. "Early Days at Old Fort Langley". BCHQ. April 1937.

Ross, Alexander. *Adventures of the First Settlers*. 1849.

Sage, W.N. "Life as a Fur Trading Post in British Columbia". WHQ. 1934.

Scholefield, E.O.S. and F.W. Howay. *British Columbia from the Earliest Times to the Present*. 1914.

Suttles, Wayne. *Coast Salish Essays*. 1987.

Tolmie, W.F. Correspondence from Fort Nisqually with James Douglas.- BCARS.

Christ Church Cathedral (Victoria). Register of Births, Deaths and Marriages.

Walbran, J.T. *British Columbia Coast Names*. 1909.

Work, John. Journal of a Voyage from Fort George to the Northward, 1824. BCARS.

Yale, J.M. Correspondence. BCARS.

Fort Langley today. The white-washed store and blacksmith shop seen from the Big House.

Friends of the Fort

Fort Langley National Historic Park
Cooperatin Association

The Friends of the Fort is a non-profit society working in cooperation with the *Fort Langley National Historic Park*. Our goal is to enhance and promote the NHP through the various events and projects that we are involved in.

The Goals of *The Friends of the Fort* are:

To provide funds and resources for projects aimed at enhancing the Park.

To promote and organize special events that correspond to the themes and objectives of the Park.

To foster the protection and longevity of the Park.

To provide and publish materials relevant to the Historic Fort.

To work with Parks Canada in the operation of a sales outlet at the Park.

To accept donations that further the cause of our society.

The Friends of the Fort
P.O. Box 1127
Fort Langley, B.C.
V0X 1J0
(604) 888-3943